THE LITTLE COLONEL: MAID OF HONOR

"LLOYD . . . TOOK HER PLACE BESIDE THE HARP"

(See page 68)

The Little Colonel: Maid of Honor

By ANNIE FELLOWS JOHNSTON

Author of "The Little Colonel Series," "Big Brother,"
"Ole Mammy's Torment," "Joel: A Boy of Galilee."
"Asa Holmes," etc.

Illustrated by ETHELDRED B. BARRY

A FIREBIRD PRESS BOOK

PELICAN PUBLISHING COMPANY
Gretna 1998

Manufactured in the United States of America

Published by Pelican Publishing Company, Inc.
1000 Burmaster Street, Gretna, Louisiana 70053

CONTENTS

CHAPTER   **PAGE**

    I. AT WARWICK HALL   1

   II. AT WARE'S WIGWAM   19

  III. IN BEAUTY'S QUEST   31

  IV. MARY'S " PROMISED LAND "   43

   V. AT " THE LOCUSTS "   58

  VI. THE FOX AND THE STORK   70

 VII. THE COMING OF THE BRIDE   88

VIII. AT THE BEECHES   113

  IX. " SOMETHING BLUE "   136

   X. " A COON HUNT "   158

  XI. THE FOUR - LEAVED CLOVER   178

 XII. THE WEDDING   198

XIII. DREAMS AND WARNINGS   216

XIV. A SECOND MAID OF HONOR   241

 XV. THE END OF THE HOUSE - PARTY 258

XVI. THE GOLDEN LEAF OF HONOR   275

LIST OF ILLUSTRATIONS

PAGE

"Lloyd . . . took her place beside the harp"
  (See page 68) . . . . . . *Frontispiece*

"It needed no second glance to tell him who
  she was" 20

"He was leaning forward in his chair, talking
  to Joyce" 66

"A tall, athletic figure in outing flannels" . 84

"A long-drawn 'o-o-oh' greeted the beautiful tableau" 132

"'All you girls standing with your hands
  stuck through the bars'" 163

"'They stepped in and rowed off down the
  shining waterway'" 171

"'One, two. three — *THROW!*'" 253

THE LITTLE COLONEL.
MAID OF HONOR

CHAPTER I.

AT WARWICK HALL

It was mid-afternoon by the old sun-dial that marked the hours in Warwick Hall garden; a sunny afternoon in May. The usual busy routine of school work was going on inside the great Hall, but no whisper of it disturbed the quiet of the sleepy old garden. At intervals the faint clang of the call-bell, signalling a change of classes, floated through the open windows, but no buzz of recitations reached the hedge-hidden path where Betty Lewis sat writing.

The whole picturesque place seemed as still as the palace of the Sleeping Beauty. Even the peacocks on the terraced river-front stood motionless, their resplendent tails spread out in the sun; and although the air was filled with the odor of wild plum blossoms, the breeze that bore it through the arbor where Betty sat, absorbed in her work, was so gentle that it scarcely stirred the vines around her.

With her elbows resting on the rustic table in front of her, and one finger unconsciously twisting the lock of curly brown hair that strayed over her ear, she sat pushing her pencil rapidly across the pages of her note-book. At times she stopped to tap impatiently on the table, when the word she wanted failed to come. Then she would sit looking through half-closed eyes at the sun-dial, or let her dreamy gaze follow the lazy windings of the river, which, far below, took its slow way along between the willows.

As editor-in-chief of *The Spinster,* there was good reason why she should be excused from recitations now and then, to spend an afternoon in this retreat. This year's souvenir volume bade fair to be the brightest and most creditable one ever issued by the school. The English professor not only openly said so, but was plainly so proud of Betty's ability that the lower classes regarded her with awe, and adored her from a distance, as a real live genius.

Whether she was a genius or not, one thing is certain, she spent hours of patient, painstaking work to make her writing measure up to the standard she had set for it. It was work that she loved better than play, however, and to-day she sighed regretfully when the hunter's horn, blowing on the upper terrace, summoned the school to its outdoor sports.

Instantly, in answer to the winding call, the whole place began to awaken. There was a tread of many feet on the great staircase, the outer doors burst open, and a stream of rollicking girls poured out into the May sunshine.

Betty knew that in a few minutes the garden would be swarming with them as if a flock of chattering magpies had taken possession of it. With a preoccupied frown drawing her eyebrows together, she began gathering up her papers, preparatory to making her escape. She glanced down the long flight of marble steps leading to the river. There on the lowest terrace, a fringe of willow-trees trailed their sweeping branches in the water. Around the largest of these trees ran a circular bench. Seated on the far side of this, the huge trunk would shield her from view of the Hall, and she decided to go down there to finish.

It would never do to stop now, when the verses were spinning themselves out so easily. None of the girls, except her four most intimate friends, would dare think of following her down there, and if she could slip away from that audacious quartette, she would be safe for the rest of the afternoon.

Peering through a hole in the hedge, she stood waiting for them to pass. A section of the botany class came first, swinging their baskets, and bound for a wooded hillside where wild flowers grew in profusion. A group on their way to the golf links came next, then half a dozen tennis players, and the newly organized basket-ball team. A moment more, and the four she was waiting for tramped out abreast, arm in arm: Lloyd Sherman, Gay Melville, Allison and Kitty Walton. Gay carried a kodak, and, from the remarks which floated over the hedge, it was evident they were on their way to the orchard, to take a picture which would illustrate the nonsense rhyme Kitty was chanting at the top of her voice. They all repeated it after her in a singsong chorus, the four pairs of feet keeping time in a soldierly tread as they marched past the garden:

" Diddledy diddledy dumpty !
Three old maids in a plum-tree !
Half a crown to get them down,
Diddledy diddledy dumpty ! "

Only in this instance Betty knew they were to
be young maids instead of old ones, all in a row
on the limb of a plum-tree in the orchard, their
laughing faces thrust through the mass of snowy
blossoms, as they waited to be photographed.

" Diddledy diddledy dumpty " — the ridiculous
refrain grew fainter and died away as the girls
passed on to the orchard, and Betty, smiling in
sympathy with their high spirits, ran down the
stately marble steps to the seat under the willow.
It was so cool and shadowy down there that at
first it was a temptation just to sit and listen to
the lap of the water against the shore, but the very
length of the shadows warned her that the afternoon was passing, and after a few moments she
fell to work again with conscientious energy.

So deeply did she become absorbed in her task,
she did not look up when some one came down the
steps behind her. It was an adoring little freshman, who had caught the glimmer of her pink
dress behind the tree. The special-delivery letter
she carried was her excuse for following. She

had been in a flutter of delight when Madame Chartley put it in her hand, asking her to find Elizabeth Lewis and give it to her. But now that she stood in the charmed presence, actually watching a poem in the process of construction, she paused, overwhelmed by the feeling that she was rushing in " where angels feared to tread."

Still, special-delivery letters are important things. Like time and tide they wait for no man. Somebody might be dead or dying. So summoning all her courage, she cleared her throat. Then she gave a bashful little cough. Betty looked up with an absent-minded stare. She had been so busy polishing a figure of speech to her satisfaction that she had forgotten where she was. For an instant the preoccupied little pucker between her eyebrows smote the timid freshman with dismay. She felt that she had gained her idol's everlasting displeasure by intruding at such a time. But the next instant Betty's face cleared, and the brown eyes smiled in the way that always made her friends wherever she went.

" What is it, Dora? " she asked, kindly. Dora, who could only stammer an embarrassed reply, held out the letter. Then she stood with toes turned in, and both hands fumbling nervously with her belt ribbon, while Betty broke the seal.

"I — I hope it isn't bad news," she managed to say at last. "I — I'd hate to bring *you* bad news."

Betty looked up with a smile which brought Dora's heart into her throat. "Thank you, dear," she answered, cordially. Then, as her eye travelled farther down the page, she gave a cry of pleasure.

"Oh, it is perfectly lovely news, Dora. It's the most beautiful surprise for Lloyd's birthday that ever was. She's not to know till to-morrow. It's too good a secret to keep to myself, so I'll share it with you in a minute if you'll swear not to tell till to-morrow."

Scarcely believing that she heard aright, Dora dropped down on the grass, regardless of the fact that her roommate and two other girls were waiting on the upper terrace for her to join them. They were going to Mammy Easter's cabin to have their fortunes told. Feeling that this was the best fortune that had befallen her since her arrival at Warwick Hall, and sure that Mammy Easter could foretell no greater honor than she was already enjoying, she signalled wildly for them to go on without her.

At first they did not understand her frantic gestures for them to go on, and stood beckoning, till she turned her back on them. Then they moved away reluctantly and in great disgust at her abandoning them. When a glance over her shoulder assured her that she was rid of them, she settled down with a blissful sigh. What greater honor could she have than to be chosen as the confidante of the most brilliant pupil ever enrolled at Warwick Hall? At least it was reported that that was the faculty's opinion of her. Dora's roommate, Cornie Dean, had chosen Lloyd Sherman as the shrine of her young affections, and it was from Cornie that Dora had learned the personal history of her literary idol. She knew that Lloyd Sherman's mother was Betty's godmother, and that the two girls lived together as sisters in a beautiful old home in Kentucky called " The Locusts." She had seen the photograph of the place hanging in Betty's room, and had heard scraps of information about the various house-parties that had frolicked under the hospitable rooftree of the fine old mansion. She knew that they had travelled abroad, and had had all sorts of delightful and unusual experiences. Now something else fine and unusual was about to happen, and Betty had offered to share a secret with her. A little shiver of pleasure passed over her at the thought. This was so delightfully intimate and confidential, almost like taking one of those "little journeys to the homes of famous people."

As Betty turned the page, Dora felt with another thrill that that was the hand which had written the poem on "Friendship," which all the girls had raved over. She herself knew it by heart, and she knew of at least six copies which, cut from the school magazine in which it had been published, were stuck in the frames of as many mirrors.

And that was the hand that had written the junior class song and the play that the juniors gave on Valentine night. If reports were true that was also the hand which would write the valedictory next year, and which was now secretly at work upon a book which would some day place its owner in the ranks with George Eliot and Thackeray.

While she still gazed in a sort of fascination at the daintily manicured pink-tipped fingers, Betty looked up with a radiant face. "Now I'll read it aloud," she said. "It will take several readings to make me realize that such a lovely time is actually in store for us. It's from godmother," she explained.

" DEAR ELIZABETH : — As I cannot be sure just when this will reach Warwick Hall, I am sending the enclosed letter to Lloyd in your care. A little package for her birthday has already gone on to her by express, but as this bit of news will give her more pleasure than any gift, I want her to receive it also on her birthday. I have just completed arrangements for a second house-party, a duplicate of the one she had six years ago, when she was eleven. I have bidden to it the same guests which came to the first one, you and Eugenia Forbes and Joyce Ware, but Eugenia will come as a bride this time. I have persuaded her to have her wedding here at Locust, among her only kindred, instead of in New York, where she and her father have no home ties. It will be a rose wedding, the last of June. The bridegroom's brother, Phil Tremont, is to be best man, and Lloyd maid of honor. Stuart's best friend, a young doctor from Boston, is to be one of the attendants, and Rob another. You and Joyce are to be bridesmaids, just as you would have been had the wedding been in New York.

"Eugenia writes that she bought the material in Paris for your gowns. I enclose a sample, pale pink chiffon. Like a rose-leaf, is it not? Dressed in this dainty color, you will certainly carry out my idea of a rose wedding. Now do not let the thoughts of all this gaiety interfere with your studies. That is all I can tell you now, but you may spend your spare time until school is out planning things to make this the happiest of house-parties, and we will try to carry out all the plans that are practicable. Your devoted godmother,

"ELIZABETH SHERMAN."

Betty spread the sample of chiffon out over her knee, and stroked it admiringly, before she slipped it back into the envelope with the letter. "The Princess is going to be so happy over this," she exclaimed. "I'm sure she'll enjoy this second house-party at seventeen a hundred times more than she did the first one at eleven, and yet nobody could have had more fun than we did at that time."

Dora's eager little face was eloquent with interest. Betty could not have chosen a more attentive listener, and, inspired by her flattering attention, she went on to recall some of the good times they had had at Locust, and in answer to Dora's timid questions explained why Lloyd was called **The Little Colonel** and the Princess Winsome and the Queen of Hearts and Hildegarde, and all the other titles her different friends had showered upon her.

" She must have been born with a gold spoon in her mouth, to be so lucky," sighed Dora, presently. " Life has been all roses for her, and no thorns whatever."

" No, indeed! " answered Betty, quickly. " She had a dreadful disappointment last year. She was taken sick during the Christmas vacation, and had to stay out of school all last term. It nearly broke her heart to drop behind her class, and she still grieves over it every day. The doctors forbade her taking extra work to catch up with it. Then so much is expected of an only child like her, who has had so many advantages, and it is no easy matter living up to all the expectations of a family like the old Colonel's."

Betty's back was turned to the terraces, but Dora, who faced them, happened to look up just then. " There she comes now," she cried in alarm. " Hide the letter! Quick, or she'll see you! "

Glancing over her shoulder, Betty saw, not only the four girls she had run away from, but four others, running down the terraces, taking the flight of marble steps two at a time. Gay's shoe-strings were tripping her at every leap, and Lloyd's hair had shaken down around her shoulders in a shining mass in the wild race from the orchard.

Lloyd reached the willow first. Dropping down on the bench, almost breathless, she began fanning herself with her hat.

"Oh!" she gasped. "Tell me quick, Betty! What is the mattah? Cornie Dean said a messenger boy had just come out to the Hall on a bicycle with a special-delivery lettah from home. I was so suah something awful had happened I could hardly run, it frightened me so."

"And we thought maybe something had happened at 'The Beeches,'" interrupted Allison, "and that mamma had written to you to break the news to us."

"Why, nothing at all is the matter," answered Betty, calmly, darting a quick look at Dora to see if her face was betraying anything. "It was just a little note from godmother. She wanted me to attend to something for her."

"But why should she send it by special delivery if it isn't impawtant?" asked Lloyd, in an aggrieved tone.

"It is important," laughed Betty. "Very."

"For goodness' sake, what is it, then?" demanded Lloyd. "Don't tease me by keeping me in suspense, Betty. You know that anything about mothah or The Locusts must concern me, too, and that I am just as much interested in the special lettah as you are. I should think it would be just as much my business as yoah's."

"This does concern you," admitted Betty, "and I'm dying to tell you, but godmother doesn't want you to know until to-morrow."

"To-morrow," echoed Lloyd, much puzzled. Then her face lighted up. "Oh, it's about my birthday present. Tell me what it is *now*, Betty," she wheedled. "I'd lots rathah know now than to wait. I could be enjoying the prospect of having whatevah it is all the rest of the day."

Betty clapped her hands over her mouth, and rocked back and forth on the bench, her eyes shining mischievously.

"*Do* go away," she begged. "*Don't* ask me! It's so lovely that I can hardly keep from telling you, and I'm afraid if you stay here I'll not have strength of character to resist."

"Tell *us*, Betty," suggested Kitty. "Lloyd will hide her ears while you confide in us."

"No, indeed!" laughed Betty. "The cat is half

out of the bag when a secret is once shared, and I
know you couldn't keep from telling Lloyd more
than an hour or two."

Just then Lloyd, leaning forward, pounced upon
something at Betty's feet. It was the sample of
pink chiffon that had dropped from the envelope.

" Sherlock Holmes the second! " she cried. " I've
discovahed the secret. It has something to do with
Eugenia's rose wedding, and mothah is going to
give me my bridesmaid's dress as a birthday present. Own up now, Betty. Isn't that it? "

Betty darted a startled look at Dora. " Well,"
she admitted, cautiously, " if it were a game of
hunt the slipper, I'd say you were getting rather
warm. That is *not* the present your mother mentioned, although it *is* a sample of the bridesmaids'
dresses. Eugenia got the material in Paris for all
of them. I'm at liberty to tell you that much."

" Is that the wedding where you are to be maid
of honor, Princess? " asked Grace Campman, one of
the girls who had been posing in the plum-tree, and
who had followed her down to hear the news.

" Yes," answered Lloyd. " Is it any wondah
that I'm neahly wild with curiosity? "

" Make her tell," urged an excited chorus. " Just
half a day beforehand won't make any difference."

"Let's all begin and beg her," suggested Grace.

Lloyd, long used to gaining her own way with Betty by a system of affectionate coaxing hard to resist, turned impulsively to begin the siege to wrest the secret from her, but another reference to the maid of honor by Grace made her pause. Then she said suddenly, with the well-known princess-like lifting of the head that they all admired:

"No, don't tell me, Betty. A maid of *honah* should be too honahable to insist on finding out things that were not intended for her to know. I hadn't thought. If mothah took all the trouble of sending a special-delivery lettah to you to keep me from knowing till my birthday, I'm not going to pry around trying to find out."

"Well, if you aren't the *queerest*," began Grace. "One would think to hear you talk that 'maid of honor' was some great title to be lived up to like the 'Maid of Orleans,' and that only some high and mighty creature like Joan of Arc could do it. But it's nothing more than to go first in the wedding march, and hold the bride's bouquet. I shouldn't think you'd let a little thing like that stand in the way of your finding out what you're so crazy to know."

"*Wouldn't* you?" asked Lloyd, with a slight

shrug, and in a tone which Dora described afterward to Cornie as simply withering.

> " ' Well, that's the difference, as you see,
> Betwixt my lord the king and *me !* ' "

To Grace's wonder, she dropped the sample of pink chiffon in Betty's lap, as if it had lost all interest for her, and stood up.

"Come on, girls," she exclaimed. " Let's take the rest of those pictuahs. There are two moah films left in the roll."

" I might as well go with you," said Betty, gathering up the loose leaves that had fallen from her note-book. " It's no use trying to write with my head so full of the grand secret. I couldn't possibly think of anything else."

Arm in arm with Allison, she sauntered up the steps behind the others to the old garden, which was the pride of every pupil in Warwick Hall. The hollyhocks from Ann Hathaway's cottage had not yet begun to flaunt their rosettes of color, but the rhododendrons from Killarney were in gorgeous bloom. As Lloyd focussed the camera in such a way as to make them a background for a picture of the sun-dial, Betty heard Kitty ask: " You'll let us know early in the morning what your present is, won't you, Princess? "

"Yes, I'll run into yoah room with it early in the mawning, just as soon as I lay eyes on it myself," promised Lloyd, solemnly.

"She can't!" whispered Betty to Allison, with a giggle. "In the first place, it's something that can't be carried, and in the second place it will take a month for her to see all of it herself."

Allison stopped short in the path, her face a picture of baffled curiosity. "Betty Lewis," she said, solemnly, "I could find it in my heart to choke you. Don't tempt me too far, or I'll do it with a good grace."

Betty laughed and pushed aside the vines at the entrance to the arbor. "Come in here," she said, in a low tone. "I've intended all along to tell you as soon as we got away from Grace Campman and those freshmen, for it concerns you and Kitty, too. You missed the first house-party we had at The Locusts, but you'll have a big share in the second one. For a June house-party with a wedding in it is the 'surprise' godmother has written about in Lloyd's birthday letter."

CHAPTER II.

AT WARE'S WIGWAM

In order that Lloyd's invitation to her own house-party might reach her on her birthday, it had not been mailed until several days after the others. So it happened that the same morning on which she slipped across the hall in her kimono, to share her first rapturous delight with Kitty, Joyce Ware's letter reached the end of its journey.

The postman on the first rural delivery route out of Phœnix jogged along in his cart toward Ware's Wigwam. He had left the highway and was following the wheel-tracks which led across the desert to Camelback Mountain. The horse dropped into a plodding walk as the wheels began pulling heavily through the sand, and the postman yawned. This stretch of road through the cactus and sage-brush was the worst part of his daily trip. He rarely passed anything more interesting than a jack-rabbit, but this morning he spied something ahead that aroused his curiosity.

At first it seemed only a flash of something pink beating the air; but, as he jogged nearer, he saw that the flash of pink was a short-skirted gingham dress. A high-peaked Mexican hat hid the face of the wearer, but it needed no second glance to tell him who she was. Every line of the sturdy little figure, from the uplifted arms brandishing a club to the dusty shoes planted widely apart to hold her balance, proclaimed that it was Mary Ware. As the blows fell with relentless energy, the postman chuckled.

"Must be killing a snake," he thought. "Whatever it is, it will be flatter than a pancake when *she* gets through with it."

Somehow he always felt like chuckling when he met Mary Ware. Whatever she happened to be doing was done with a zeal and a vim that made this fourteen-year-old girl a never-failing source of amusement to the easy-going postman. Now as he came within speaking distance, he saw a surrey drawn up to the side of the road, and recognized the horse as old Bogus from Lee's ranch.

A thin, tall woman, swathed in a blue veil, sat stiffly on the back seat, reaching forward to hold the reins in a grasp that showed both fear and unfamiliarity in the handling of horses. She was a

"IT NEEDED NO SECOND GLANCE TO TELL HIM WHO SHE WAS"

new boarder at Lee's ranch. Evidently they had been out on some errand for Mrs. Lee, and were returning from one of the neighboring orange-groves, for the back of the surrey was filled with oranges and grapefruit.

The postman's glance turned from the surrey to the object in the road with an exclamation of surprise. One of the largest rattlesnakes he had ever seen lay stretched out there, and Mary, having dropped her club, was proceeding to drag it toward the surrey by a short lasso made of a piece of the hitching-rope. The postman stood up in his cart to look at it.

" Better be sure it's plumb dead before you give it a seat in your carriage," he advised.

Mary gave a glance of disgust toward the blue-veiled figure in the surrey.

" Oh, it's *dead,*" she said, witheringly. " Mr. Craydock shot its head off to begin with, over at the orange-grove this morning, and I've killed it four different times on our way home. He gave it to me to take to Norman for his collection. But Miss Scudder is so scared of it that she makes me get out every half-mile to pound a few more inches off its neck. It was a perfect beauty when we started, — five feet long and twelve rattles. I'm

so afraid I'll break off some of the rattles that I'll
he mighty glad when I get it safely home."

"So will I!" ejaculated Miss Scudder, so fer-
vently that the postman laughed as he drove
on.

"Any mail for us?" Mary called after him.

"Only some papers and a letter for your sister,"
he answered over his shoulder.

"Now why didn't I ask him to take me and the
snake on home in the cart with him?" exclaimed
Mary, as she lifted the rattler into the surrey by
means of the lasso, and took the reins from the
new boarder's uneasy hands. "Even if you can't
drive, Bogus could take you to the ranch all right
by himself. Lots of times when Hazel Lee and I
are out driving, we wrap the reins around the whip-
holder and let him pick his own way. Now I'll
have to drag this snake all the way from the ranch
to the Wigwam, and it will be a dreadful holdback
when I'm in such a hurry to get there and see who
Joyce's letter is from.

"You see," she continued, clucking cheerfully to
Bogus, "the postman's mail-pouch is almost as
interesting as a grab-bag, since my two brothers
went away. Holland is in the navy," she added,
proudly, "and my oldest brother, Jack, has a posi-

tion in the mines up where mamma and Norman and I are going to spend the summer."

Three years in the desert had not made Mary Ware any the less talkative. At fourteen she was as much of a chatterbox as ever, but so diverting, with her fund of unexpected information and family history and her cheerful outlook on life, that Mrs. Lee often sent for her to amuse some invalid boarder, to the mutual pleasure of the small philosopher and her audience.

The experiment this morning had proved anything but a pleasure drive for either of them, however. Timid Miss Scudder, afraid of horses, afraid of the lonely desert, and with a deathly horror of snakes, gave a sigh of relief when they came in sight of the white tents clustered around the brown adobe ranch house on the edge of the irrigating canal. But with the end of her journey in sight, she relaxed her strained muscles and nerves somewhat, and listened with interest to what Mary was saying.

" This year has brought three of us our heart's desires, anyhow. Holland has been wild to get into the navy ever since he was big enough to know that there is one. Jack has been looking forward to this position in the mines ever since we came out

West. It will be the making of him, everybody says. And Joyce's one dream in life has been to save enough money to go East to take lessons in designing. Her bees have done splendidly, but I don't believe she could have *quite* managed it if Eugenia Forbes hadn't invited her to be one of the bridesmaids at her wedding, and promised to send her a pass to New York."

She broke off abruptly as Bogus came to a stop in front of the tents, and, standing up, she proceeded to dangle the snake carefully over the wheel, till it was lowered in safety to the ground. Ordinarily she would have lingered at the ranch until the occupant of every tent had strolled out to admire her trophy, and afterward might have accepted Hazel Lee's invitation to stay to dinner. It was a common occurrence for them to spend their Saturdays together. But to-day not even the promise of strawberry shortcake and a ride home afterward, when it was cooler, could tempt her to stay.

The yellow road stretched hot and glaring across the treeless desert. The snake was too heavy to carry on a pole over her shoulder. She would have to drag it through the sun and sand if she went now. But her curiosity was too strong to allow her to wait. She must find out what was in that letter to Joyce. If it were from Jack, there would be something in it about their plans for the summer; maybe a kodak picture of the shack in the pine woods near the mines, where they were to board. If it were from Holland, there would be another interesting chapter of his experiences on board the training-ship.

Once as she trudged along the road, it occurred to her that the letter might be from her cousin Kate, the " witch with a wand," who had so often played fairy godmother to the family. She might be writing to say that she had sent another box. Straightway Mary's active imagination fell to picturing its contents so blissfully that she forgot the heat of the sun-baked road over which she was going. Her face was beaded with perspiration and her eyes squinted nearly shut under the broad brim of the Mexican sombrero, but, revelling in the picture her mind called up of cool white dresses and dainty thin-soled slippers, she walked faster and faster, oblivious to the heat and the glaring light. Her sunburned cheeks were flaming red when she finally reached the Wigwam, and the locks of hair straggling down her forehead hung in limp wet strings.

Lifting the snake carefully across the bridge

which spanned the irrigating canal, she trailed it into the yard and toward the umbrella-tree which shaded the rustic front porch. Under this sheltering umbrella-tree, which spread its dense arch like a roof, sat Joyce and her mother. The heap of muslin goods piled up around them showed that they had spent a busy morning sewing. But they were idle now. One glance showed Mary that the letter, whosever it was, had brought unusual news. Joyce sat on the door-step with it in her lap and her hands clasped over her knees. Mrs. Ware, leaning back in her sewing-chair, was opening and shutting a pair of scissors in an absent-minded manner, as if her thoughts were a thousand miles away.

" Well, it's good news, anyway," was Mary's first thought, as she glanced at her sister's radiant face. " She wouldn't look so pretty if it wasn't. It's a pity she can't be hearing good news all the time. When her eyes shine like that, she's almost beautiful. Now me, all the good news in the world wouldn't make *me* look beautiful, freckled and fat and sunburned as I am, and my hair so fine and thin and straight — "

She paused in her musings to look up each sleeve for her handkerchief, and not finding it in either, caught up the hem of her short pink skirt to wipe her perspiring face.

"Oh, *what* did the postman bring?" she demanded, seating herself on the edge of the hammock swung under the umbrella-tree. "I've almost walked myself into a sunstroke, hurrying to get here and find out. Is it from Jack or Holland or Cousin Kate?"

"It is from The Locusts," answered Joyce, leaning forward to see what was tied to the other end of the rope which Mary still held. Seeing that it was only a snake, something which Mary and Holland were always dragging home, to add to their collection of skins and shells, she went on:

"The Little Colonel is to have a second house-party. The same girls that were at the first one are invited for the month of June, and Eugenia is to be married there instead of in New York. Think what a wedding it will be, in that beautiful old Southern home! A thousand times nicer than it would have been in New York."

She stopped to enjoy the effect her news had produced. Mary's face was glowing with unselfish pleasure in her sister's good fortune.

"And we're to wear pale pink chiffon dresses, just the color of wild roses. Eugenia got the material in Paris when she ordered her wedding-gown, and they're to be made in Louisville after we get there."

The light in Mary's face was deepening.

"And Phil Tremont is to be there the entire month of June. He is to be best man, you know, since Eugenia is to marry his brother."

"Oh, Joyce!" gasped Mary. "What a heavenly time you are going to have! Just The Locusts by itself would be good enough, but to be there at a house-party, and have Phil there and to see a wedding! I've always wanted to go to a wedding. I never saw one in my life."

"Tell her the rest, daughter," prompted Mrs. Ware, gently. "Don't keep her in the dark any longer."

"Well, then," said Joyce, smiling broadly. "Let me break it to you by degrees, so the shock won't give you apoplexy or heart-failure. The rest of it is, that *you* — Mary Ware, are invited also. *You* are invited to go with me to the house-party at The Locusts! And *you'll* see the wedding, for Mr. Sherman is going to send tickets for both of us, and mamma and I have made all the plans. Now that she is so well, she won't need either of us while she's up at the camp with Jack, and the money it would have taken to pay your board will buy the new clothes you need."

All the color faded out of the hot little face as Mary listened, growing pale with excitement.

"Oh, mamma, is it *true?*" she asked, imploringly. "I don't see how it can be. But Joyce wouldn't fool me about anything as big as this, would she?"

She asked the question in such a quiver of eagerness that the tears sprang to her eyes. Joyce had expected her to spin around on her toes and squeal one delighted little squeal after another, as she usually did when particularly happy. She did not know what to expect next, when all of a sudden Mary threw herself across her mother's lap and began to sob and laugh at the same time.

"Oh, mamma, the old Vicar was right. It's been awfully hard sometimes to k-keep inflexible. Sometimes I thought it would nearly k-kill me! But we did it! We did it! And now fortune *has* changed in our favor, and everything is all right!"

A rattle of wheels made her look up and hastily wipe the hem of her pink skirt across her face again. A wagon was stopping at the gate, and the man who was to stay in one of the tents and take care of the bees in their absence was getting out to discuss the details of the arrangement. Joyce tossed the letter into Mary's lap and rose to follow her mother out to the hives. There were several matters of business to arrange with him, and Mary knew it would be some time before they could resume the exciting conversation he had interrupted. She read the letter through, hardly believing the magnitude of her good fortune. But, as the truth of it began to dawn upon her, she felt that she could not possibly keep such news to herself another instant. It might be an hour before Joyce and her mother had finished discussing business with the man and Norman was away fishing somewhere up the canal.

So, settling her hat on her head, she started back over the hot road, so absorbed in the thought of all she had to tell Hazel that she was wholly unconscious of the fact that she was still holding tightly to the rope tied around the rattler's neck. Five feet of snake twitched along behind her as she started on a run toward the ranch.

CHAPTER III

" Fortune has at last — fortune has at last —
Fortune has at last changed in our *fa*-vor ! "

A HUNDRED times, in the weeks that followed,
Mary turned the old Vicar's saying into sort of a
chant, and triumphantly intoned it as she went about
the house, making preparations for her journey.
Most of the time she was not aware that her lips
were repeating what her heart was constantly singing, and one day, to her dire mortification, she
chanted the entire strain in one of the largest dry-
goods stores in Phœnix, before she realized what
she was doing.

She had gone with Joyce to select some dress
material for herself. It had been so long since
Mary had had any clothes except garments made
over and handed down, that the wealth of choice
offered her was almost overpowering. To be sure
it was a bargain counter they were hanging over,

but the remnants of lawn and organdy and gingham were so entrancingly new in design and dainty in coloring, that without a thought to appearances she caught up the armful of pretty things which Joyce had decided they could afford. Clasping them ecstatically in an impulsive hug, she sang at the top of her voice, just as she would have done had she been out alone on the desert: "Fortune has at last changed in our *fa*-vor!"

When Joyce's horrified exclamation and the clerk's amused smile recalled her to her surroundings, she could have gone under the counter with embarrassment. Although she flushed hotly for several days whenever she thought of the way everybody in the store turned to stare at her, she still hummed the same words whenever a sense of her great good fortune overwhelmed her. Such times came frequently, especially whenever a new garment was completed and she could try it on with much preening and many satisfied turns before the mirror.

It was on one of these occasions, when she was proudly revolving in the daintiest of them all, a pale blue mull which she declared was the color of a wild morning-glory, that a remark of her mother's, in the next room, filled her with dismay. It had not been intended for her ears, but it floated in distinctly, above the whirr of the sewing-machine.

"Joyce, I am sorry we made up that blue for Mary. She's so tanned and sunburned that it seems to bring out all the red tints in her skin, and makes her look like a little squaw. I never realized how this climate has injured her complexion until I saw her in that shade of blue, and remembered how becoming it used to be. She was like an apple-blossom, all white and pink, when we came out here."

Mary had been so busy looking at her new clothes that she had paid little attention to the face above them, reflected in the mirror. It had tanned so gradually that she had become accustomed to having that sunbrowned little visage always smile back at her. Besides, every one she met was tanned by the wind and weather, some of them spotted with big dark freckles. Joyce wasn't. Joyce had always been careful about wearing a sunbonnet or a wide brimmed hat when she went out in the sun. Mary remembered now, with many compunctions, how often she had been warned to do the same. She wished with all her ardent little soul that she had not been so careless, and presently, after a serious, half-tearful study of herself in the glass, she went away to find a remedy.

In the back of the cook-book, she remembered, there was a receipt for cold cream, and in a magazine Mrs. Lee had loaned them was a whole column devoted to face bleaches and complexion restorers. Having read each formula, she decided to try them all in turn, if the first did not prove effective.

Buttermilk and lemon juice were to be had for the taking and could be applied at night after Joyce had gone to sleep. Half-ashamed of this desire to make herself beautiful, Mary shrank from confiding her troubles to any one. But several nights' use of all the home remedies she could get, failed to produce the desired results. When she anxiously examined herself in the glass, the unflattering mirror plainly showed her a little face, not one whit fairer for all its treatment.

The house-party was drawing near too rapidly to waste time on things of such slow action, and at last, in desperation, she took down the savings-bank in which, after long hoarding, she had managed to save nearly two dollars. By dint of a button-hook and a hat-pin and an hour's patient poking, she succeeded in extracting five dimes. These she wrapped in tissue paper, and folded in a letter. In a Phœnix newspaper she had seen an advertisement of a magical cosmetic, to be found on sale at one of the local drug-stores, and this was an order for a box.

She was accustomed to running out to watch for the postman. Often in her eagerness to get the mail she had met him half a mile down the road. So she had ample opportunity to send her order and receive a reply without the knowledge of any of the family.

It was a delicious-smelling ointment. The directions on the wrapper said that on retiring, it was to be applied to the face like a thick paste, and a linen mask worn to prevent its rubbing off.

Now that the boys were away, Mary shared the circular tent with Joyce. The figures " mystical and awful " which she and Holland had put on its walls with green paint the day they moved to the Wigwam, had faded somewhat in the fierce sun of tropical summers, but they still grinned hideously from all sides. Outlandish as they were, however, no face on all the encircling canvas was as grotesque as the one which emerged from under the bed late in the afternoon, the day the box of cosmetic was received.

Mary had crept under the bed in order to escape Norman's prying eyes in case he should glance into the tent in search of her. There, stretched out on the floor with a pair of scissors and a piece of one of her old linen aprons, she had fashioned herself a mask, in accordance with the directions on the box. The holes cut for the eyes and nose were a trifle irregular, one eye being nearly half an inch higher than the other, and the mouth was decidedly askew. But tapes sewed on at the four corners made it ready for instant use, and when she had put it on and crawled out from under the bed, she regarded herself in the glass with great satisfaction.

" I hope Joyce won't wake up in the night and see me," she thought. " She'd be scared stiff. This is a lot of trouble and expense, but I just can't go to the house-party looking like a fright. I'd do lots more than this to keep the Princess from being ashamed of me."

Then she put it away and went out to the hammock, under the umbrella-tree, and while she sat swinging back and forth for a long happy hour, she pictured to herself the delights of the coming house-party. The Princess would be changed, she knew. Her last photograph showed that. One is almost grown up at seventeen, and she had been only four-teen, Mary's age, when she made that never to be forgotten visit to the Wigwam. And she would see Betty and Betty's godmother and Papa Jack and the old Colonel and Mom Beck. The very names, as she repeated them in a whisper, sounded interesting to her. And the two little knights of Kentucky, and Miss Allison and the Waltons—they were all mythical people in one sense, like Alice in Wonderland and Bo-peep, yet in another they were as real as Holland or Hazel Lee, for they were household names, and she had heard so much about them that she felt a sort of kinship with each one.

With the mask and the box tucked away in readiness under her pillow, it was an easy matter after Joyce had gone to sleep for Mary to lift herself to a sitting posture, inch by inch. Cautiously as a cat she raised herself, then sat there in the darkness scooping out the smooth ointment with thumb and finger, and spreading it thickly over her inquisitive little nose and plump round cheeks. All up under her hair and down over her chin she rubbed it with energy and thoroughness. Then tying on the mask, she eased herself down on her elbow, little by little, and snuggled into her pillow with a sigh of relief.

It was a long time before she fell asleep. The odor of the ointment was sickeningly sweet, and the mask gave her a hot smothery feeling. When she finally dozed off it was to fall into a succession of uneasy dreams. She thought that the cat was sitting on her face; that an old ogre had her head tied up in a bag and was carrying it home to change into an apple dumpling, then that she was a fly and had fallen into a bottle of mucilage. From the last dream she roused with a start, hot and uncomfortable, but hardly wide awake enough to know what was the matter.

The salty dried beef they had had for supper made her intensely thirsty, and remembering the pitcher of fresh water which Joyce always brought into the tent every night, she slipped out of bed and stumbled across the floor toward the table. The moon was several nights past the full now, so that at this late hour the walls of the tent glimmered white in its light, and where the flap was turned back at the end, it shone in, in a broad white path.

Not more than half awake, Mary had forgotten the elaborate way in which she had tied up her face, and catching sight in the mirror of an awful spook gliding toward her, she stepped back, almost frozen with terror. Never had she imagined such a hideous ghost, white as flour, with one round eye higher than the other, and a dreadful slit of a mouth, all askew.

She was too frightened to utter a sound, but the pitcher fell to the floor with a crash, and as the cold water splashed over her feet she bounded back into bed and pulled the cover over her head. Instantly, as her hand came in contact with the mask on her face, she realized that it was only her own reflection in the glass which had frightened her, but the shock was so great she could not stop trembling.

Wakened by the sound of the breaking pitcher and Mary's wild plunge back into bed, Joyce sat up in alarm, but in response to her whisper Mary explained in muffled tones from under the bedclothes that she had simply gotten up for a drink of water and dropped the pitcher. All the rest of the night her sleep was fitful and uneasy, for toward morning her face began to burn as if it were on fire. She tore off the mask and used it to wipe away what remained of the ointment. Most of it had been absorbed, however, and the skin was broken out in little red blisters.

Maybe in her zeal she had used too much of the magical cosmetic, or maybe her face, already made tender by various applications, resented the vigorous rubbings she gave it. At any rate she had cause to be frightened when she saw herself in the mirror. As she lifted the pitcher from the washstand, she happened to glance at the proverb calendar hanging over the towel-rack, and saw the verse

for the day. It was " Pride goeth before destruc-
tion, and a haughty spirit before a fall." The big
red letters stood out accusingly.

" Oh dear," she thought, as she plunged her burning face into the bowl of cold water, " if I hadn't
had so much miserable pride, I wouldn't have des-
troyed what little complexion I had left. Like as
not the skin will all peel off now, and I'll look like a
half-scaled fish for weeks."

She was so irritable later, when Joyce exclaimed
over her blotched and mottled appearance, that Mrs.
Ware decided she must be coming down with some
kind of rash. It was only to prevent her mother
sending for a doctor, that Mary finally confessed
with tears what she had done.

" Why didn't you ask somebody? " said Joyce,
trying not to let her voice betray the laughter which
was choking her, for Mary showed a grief too deep
to ridicule.

" I — I was ashamed to," she confessed, " and I
wanted to surprise you all. The advertisement said
g-grow b-beautiful while you sleep, and now — oh,
it's *spoiled* me! " she wailed. " And I can't go to
the house-party — "

" Yes, you can, goosey," said Joyce, consolingly.
" Mamma has Grandma Ware's old receipt for rose

balm, that will soon heal those blisters. You would have saved yourself a good deal of trouble and suffering if you had gone to her in the first place."

"Well, don't I know that?" blazed Mary, angrily. Then hiding her face in her arms she began to sob. "You don't know what it is to be uh-ugly like me! I heard mamma say that I was as brown as a squaw, and I couldn't bear to think of Lloyd and Betty and everybody at The Locusts seeing me that way. *That's* why I did it!"

"You are not ugly, Mary Ware," insisted Joyce, in a most reproving big-sisterly voice. "Everybody can't be a raving, tearing beauty, and anybody with as bright and attractive a little face as yours ought to be satisfied to let well enough alone."

"That's all right for *you*," replied Mary, bitterly. "But you aren't fat, with a turned-up nose and just a little thin straight pigtail of hair. "You're pretty, and an artist, and you're going to be somebody some day. But I'm just plain 'little Mary,' with no talents or *anything!*"

Choking with tears, she rushed out of the room, and took refuge in the swing down by the beehives. For once the "School of the Bees" failed to whisper a comforting lesson. This was a trouble which she could not seal up in its cell, and for many days it poisoned all life's honey. Presently she slipped back into the house for a pencil and box of paper, and sitting on the swing with her geography on her knees for a writing-table, she poured out her troubles in a letter to Jack. It was only a few hundred miles to the mines, and she could be sure of a sympathetic answer before the blisters were healed on her face, or the hurt had faded out of her sensitive little heart.

CHAPTER IV.

MARY'S " PROMISED LAND "

IT was a hot, tiresome journey back to Kentucky. Joyce, worn out with all the hurried preparations of packing her mother and Norman off to the mines, closing the Wigwam for the summer, and putting her own things in order for a long absence, was glad to lean back in her seat with closed eyes, and take no notice of her surroundings. But Mary travelled in the same energetic way in which she killed snakes. Nothing escaped her. Every passenger in the car, every sight along the way was an object of interest. She sat up straight and eager, scarcely batting an eyelash, for fear of missing something.

To her great relief the peeling process had been a short one, and thanks to the rose balm, not a trace of a blister was left on her smooth skin to remind her of her foolish little attempt to beautify herself in secret. The first day she made no acquaintances for she admired the reserved way in which her pretty nineteen-year-old sister travelled, and tried to imitate her, but after one day of elegant composure she longed for a chance to drop into easy sociability with some of her neighbors. They no longer seemed like strangers after she had travelled in their company for twenty-four hours.

So she seized the first social opportunity which came to her next morning. A middle-aged woman, who was taking up all the available space in the dressing-room, grudgingly moved over a few inches when Mary tried to squeeze in to wash her face. Any one but Mary would have regarded her as a most unpromising companion, when she answered her question with a grumbling " Yes, been on two days, and got two more to go." The tone was as ungracious as if she had said, " Mind your own business."

The train was passing over a section of rough road just then, and they swayed against each other several times, with polite apologies on Mary's part. Then as the woman finished skewering her hair into a tight knot she relaxed into friendliness far enough to ask, " Going far yourself? "

" Yes, indeed! " answered Mary, cheerfully, reaching for a towel. " Going to the Promised Land."

The car gave a sudden lurch, and the woman

dropped her comb, as she was sent toppling against Mary so forcibly that she pinned her to the wall a moment.

" My ! " she exclaimed as she regained her balance. " You don't mean clear to Palestine ! "

" No'm; our promised land is Kentucky," Mary hastened to explain. " Mamma used to live there, and she's told us so much about the beautiful times that she used to have in Lloydsboro Valley that it's been the dream of our life to go there. Since we've been wandering around in the desert, sort of camping out the way the old Israelites did, we've got into the way of calling that our promised land."

" Well, I wouldn't count too much on it," advised the woman, sourly. " They say distance lends enchantment, and things hardly ever turn out as nice as you think they're going to."

" They do at our house," persisted Mary, with unfailing cheerfulness. " They generally turn out nicer."

Evidently her companion felt the worse for a night in a sleeper and had not yet been set to rights with the world by her morning cup of coffee, for she answered as if Mary's rose-colored view of life so early in the day irritated her.

" Well, maybe your folks are an exception to the

rule," she said, sharply, " but I know how it is with the world in general. Even old Moses himself didn't have his journey turn out the way he expected to. He looked forward to *his* promised land for forty years, and then didn't get to put foot on it."

" But he got to go to heaven instead," persisted Mary, triumphantly, " and that's the best thing that could happen to anybody, especially if you're one hundred and twenty years old."

There was no answer to this statement, and another passenger appearing at the dressing-room door just then, the woman remarked something about two being company and three a crowd, and squeezed past Mary to let the newcomer take her place.

" *She* was more crowd than company," remarked Mary confidentially to the last arrival. " She took up most as much room as two people, and it's awful the way she looks on the dark side of things."

There was an amused twinkle in the newcomer's eyes. She was a much younger woman than the one whose place she had taken, and evidently it was no trial for her to be sociable before breakfast. In a few minutes she knew all about the promised land to which the little pilgrim was journeying, and showed such friendly interest in the wedding and the other delights in store for her that Mary lingered over her toilet as long as possible, in order to prolong the pleasure of having such an attentive audience.

But she found others just as attentive before the day was over. The grateful mother whose baby she played with, welcomed her advances as she would have welcomed sunshine on a rainy day. The tired tourists who yawned over their time-tables, found her enthusiastic interest in everybody the most refreshing thing they had met in their travels. By night she was on speaking terms with nearly everybody in the car, and at last, when the long journey was done, a host of good wishes and good-byes followed her all down the aisle, as her new-made friends watched her departure, when the train slowed into the Union Depot in Louisville. She little dreamed what an apostle of good cheer she had been on her journey, or how long her eager little face and odd remarks would be remembered by her fellow passengers.

All she thought of as the train stopped was that at last she had reached her promised land.

Those of the passengers who had thrust their heads out of the windows, saw a tall, broad-shouldered young man come hurrying along toward the girls, and heard Joyce exclaim in surprise, " Why, Rob Moore! Who ever dreamed of seeing *you* here? I thought you were in college? "

" So I was till day before yesterday," he answered, as they shook hands like the best of old friends. " But grandfather was so ill they telegraphed for me, and I got leave of absence for the rest of the term. We were desperately alarmed about him, but ' all's well that ends well.' He is out of danger now, and it gave me this chance of coming to meet you."

Mary, standing at one side, watched in admiring silence the easy grace of his greeting and the masterful way in which he took possession of Joyce's suit-case and trunk checks. When he turned to her to acknowledge his introduction as respectfully as if she had been forty instead of fourteen, her admiration shot up like mercury in a thermometer. She had felt all along that she knew Rob Moore intimately, having heard so much of his past escapades from Joyce and Lloyd. It was Rob who had given Joyce the little fox terrier, Bob, which had been such a joy to the whole family. It was Rob who had shared all the interesting life at The Locusts which she had heard pictured so vividly that she had long felt that she even knew exactly how he looked.

It was somewhat of a shock to find him grown up into this dignified young fellow, broad of shoulders and over six feet tall.

As he led the way out to the street and hailed a passing car, he explained why Lloyd had not come in to meet them, adding, " Your train was two hours late, so I telephoned out to Mrs. Sherman that we would have lunch in town. I'll take you around to Benedict's."

Mary had never eaten in a restaurant before, so it was with an inward dread that she might betray the fact that she followed Joyce and Rob to a side-table spread for three. In her anxiety to do the right thing she watched her sister like a hawk, copy-ing every motion, till they were safely launched on the first course of their lunch. Then she relaxed her watchfulness long enough to take a full breath and look at some of the people to whom Rob had bowed as they entered.

She wanted to ask the name of the lady in black at the opposite table. The little girl with her at-tracted her interest so that she could hardly eat. She was about her own age and she had such lovely long curls and such big dark eyes. To Mary, whose besetting sin was a love of pretty clothes, the picture hat the other girl wore was irresistible. She could not keep her admiring glances away from it, and she wished with all her heart she had one like it. Presently Joyce noticed it too, and asked the very question Mary had been longing to ask.

"That is Mrs. Walton, the General's wife, you know," answered Rob, "and her youngest daughter, Elise. You'll probably see all three of the girls while you're at The Locusts, for they're living in the Valley now and are great friends of Lloyd and Betty."

"Oh, I know all about them," answered Joyce, "for Allison and Kitty go to Warwick Hall, and Lloyd and Betty fill their letters with their sayings and doings." Mary stole another glance at the lady in black. So this was an aunt of the two little knights of Kentucky, and the mother of the "Little Captain," whose name had been in all the papers as the youngest commissioned officer in the entire army. She would have something to tell Holland in her next letter. He had always been so interested in everything pertaining to Ranald Walton, and had envied him his military career until he himself had an opportunity to go into the navy.

Presently Mrs. Walton finished her lunch, and on her way out stopped at their table to shake hands with Rob.

"I was sure that this is Joyce Ware and her sister," she exclaimed, cordially, as Rob introduced them. "My girls are so excited over your coming they can hardly wait to meet you. They are having a little house-party themselves, at present, some girls from Lexington and two young army officers, whom I want you to know. Come here, Elise, and meet the Little Colonel's Wild West friends. Oh, we've lived in Arizona too, you know," she added, laughing, "and I've a thousand questions to ask you about our old home. I'm looking forward to a long, cozy toe-to-toe on the subject, every time you come to The Beeches."

After a moment's pleasant conversation she passed on, leaving such an impression of friendly cordiality that Joyce said, impulsively, "She's just *dear!* She makes you feel as if you'd known her always. Now toe-to-toe, for instance. That's lots more intimate and sociable than tête-à-tête."

"That's what I thought, too," exclaimed Mary. "And isn't it nice, when you come visiting this way, to know everybody's history beforehand! Then just as soon as they appear on the scene you can fit in a background behind them."

It was the first remark Mary had made in Rob's hearing, except an occasional monosyllable in regard to her choice of dishes on the bill of fare, and he turned to look at her with an amused smile, as if he had just waked up to the fact that she was present.

" She's a homely little thing," he thought, " but she looks as if she might grow up to be diverting company. She couldn't be a sister of Joyce's and not be bright." Then, in order to hear what she might say, he began to ask her questions. She was eating ice-cream. Joyce, who had refused dessert on account of a headache, opened her chatelaine bag to take out an envelope already stamped and addressed.

" If you'll excuse me while you finish your cof-**fee**," she said to Rob, " I'll scribble a line to mamma to let her know we've arrived safely. I've dropped notes all along the way, but this is the one she'll be waiting for most anxiously. It will take only a minute."

" Certainly," answered Rob, looking at his watch. " We have over twenty minutes to catch the next trolley out to the Valley. They run every half-hour now, you know. So take your time. It will give me a chance to talk to Mary. She hasn't told me yet what her impressions are of this grand old **Commonwealth**."

If he had thought his teasing tone would bring the color to her face, it was because he was not as familiar with her background as she was with his. A long apprenticeship under Jack and Holland had made her proof against ordinary banter.

" Well," she began, calmly, mashing the edges of her ice-cream with her spoon to make it melt faster, " so far it is just as I imagined it would be. I've always thought of Kentucky as a place full of colored people and pretty girls and polite men. Of course I've not been anywhere yet but just in this room, and it certainly seems to be swarming with colored waiters. I can't see all over the room without turning around, but the ladies at the tables in front of me and the ones reflected in the mirrors are good-looking and stylish. Those girls you bowed to over there are pretty enough to be Gibson girls, just stepped out of a magazine; and so far — *you* are the only man I have met."

" Well," he said after a moment's waiting, " you haven't given me your opinion of *me.*"

There was a quizzical twinkle in his eye, which Mary, intent upon her beloved ice-cream, did not see. Her honest little face was perfectly serious as she replied, " Oh, *you,* — you're like Marse Phil and Marse Chan and those men in Thomas Nelson

Page's stories of ' Ole Virginia.' I love those stories, don't you? Especially the one about ' Meh Lady.' Of course I know that everybody in the South can't be as nice as they are, but whenever I think of Kentucky and Virginia I think of people like that."

Such a broad compliment was more than Rob was prepared for. An embarrassed flush actually crept over his handsome face. Joyce, glancing up, saw it and laughed.

" Mary is as honest as the father of his country himself," she said. " I'll warn you now. She'll always tell exactly what she thinks."

" Now, Joyce," began Mary, indignantly, " you know I don't tell everything I think. I'll admit that I did use to be a chatterbox, when I was little, but even Holland says I'm not, now."

" I didn't mean to call you a chatterbox," explained Joyce. " I was just warning Rob that he must expect perfectly straightforward replies to his questions."

Joyce bent over her letter, and in order to start Mary to talking again, Rob cast about for another topic of conversation.

" You wouldn't call those three girls at that last table, Gibson girls, would you? " he asked. " Look at that dark slim one with the red cherries in her hat."

Mary glanced at her critically. "No," she said, slowly. "She is not exactly pretty now, but she's the ugly-duckling kind. She may turn out to be the most beautiful swan of them all. I like that the best of any of Andersen's fairy tales. Don't you? I used to look at myself in the glass and tell myself that it would be that way with me. That my straight hair and pug nose needn't make any difference; that some day I'd surprise people as the ugly duckling did. But Jack said, no, I am not the swan kind. That no amount of waiting will make straight hair curly and a curly nose straight. Jack says I'll have my innings when I am an old lady — that I'll not be pretty till I'm old. Then he says I'll make a beautiful grandmother, like Grandma Ware. He says her face was like a benediction. That's what he wrote to me just before I left home. Of course I'd rather be a beauty than a benediction, any day. But Jack says he laughs best who laughs last, and it's something to look forward to, to know you're going to be nice-looking in your old age when all your friends are wrinkled and faded."

Rob's laugh was so appreciative that Mary felt with a thrill that he was finding her really entertaining. She was sorry that Joyce's letter came to an end just then. Her mother's last warning had been for her to remember on all occasions that she was much younger than Joyce's friends, and they would not expect her to take a grown-up share of their conversation. She had promised earnestly to try to curb her active little tongue, no matter how much she wanted to be chief spokesman, and now, remembering her promise, she relapsed into sudden silence.

All the way out to the Valley she sat with her hands folded in her lap, on the seat opposite Joyce and Rob. The car made so much noise she could catch only an occasional word of their conversation, so she sat looking out of the window, busy with her thoughts.

"Sixty minutes till we get there. Now it's only fifty-nine. Now it's fifty-eight — just like the song 'Ten little, nine little, eight little Indians.' Pretty soon there'll just be one minute left."

At this exciting thought the queer quivery feeling inside was so strong it almost choked her. Her heart gave a great thump when Joyce finally called, "Here we are," and Rob signalled the conductor to stop outside the great entrance gate.

"The Locusts" at last. Pewees in the cedars

and robins on the lawn; everywhere the cool deep
shadows of great trees, and wide stretches of waving blue-grass. Stately white pillars of an old
Southern mansion gleamed through the vines at the
end of the long avenue. Then a flutter of white
dresses and gay ribbons, and Lloyd and Betty came
running to meet them.

CHAPTER V.

LLOYD and Betty had been home from Warwick Hall only two days, and the joyful excitement of arrival had not yet worn off. The Locusts had never looked so beautiful to them as it did this vacation, and their enthusiasm over all that was about to happen kept them in a flutter from morning till night.

When Rob's telephone message came that the train was late and that he could not bring the girls out until after lunch, Lloyd chafed at the delay at first. Then she consoled herself with the thought that she could arrange a more effective welcome for the middle of the afternoon than for an earlier hour.

" Grandfathah will have had his nap by that time," she said, with a saucy glance in his direction, " and he will be as sweet and lovely as a May mawning. And he'll have on a fresh white suit for the evening, and a cah'nation in his button-hole." Then she gave her orders more directly.

" You must be suah to be out on the front steps to welcome them, grandfathah, with yoah co'tliest bow. And mothah, you must be beside him in that embroidered white linen dress of yoahs that I like so much. Mom Beck will stand in the doahway behind you all just like a pictuah of an old-time South'n welcome. Of co'se Joyce has seen it all befoah, but little Mary has been looking foh'wa'd to this visit to The Locusts as she would to heaven. You know what Joyce wrote about her calling this her promised land."

" I know how it is going to make her feel," said Betty. " Just as it made me feel when I got here from the Cuckoo's Nest, and found this ' House Beautiful ' of my dreams. And if she is the little dreamer that I was the best time will not be the arrival, but early candle-lighting time, when you are playing on your harp. I used to sit on a foot-stool at godmother's feet, so unutterably happy, that I would have to put out my hand to feel her dress. I was so afraid that she might vanish — that every-thing was too lovely to be real.

" And now, to think," she added, turning to Mrs. Sherman and affectionately laying a hand on each shoulder, "it's lasted all this time, till I have grown so tall that I could pick you up and carry you off, little godmother. I am going to do it some day soon, lift you up bodily and put you into a story that I have begun to write. It will be my best work, because it is what I have lived."

"You'd better live awhile longer," laughed Mrs. Sherman, "before you begin to settle what your best work will be. Think how the shy little Elizabeth of twelve has blossomed into the stately Elizabeth of eighteen, and think what possibilities are still ahead of you in the next six years."

"When mothah and Betty begin to compliment each othah," remarked Lloyd, seating herself on the arm of the old Colonel's chair, "they are lost to all else in the world. So while we have this moment to ou'selves, my deah grandfathah, I want to impress something on yoah mind, very forcibly."

The playful way in which she held him by the ears was a familiarity no one but Lloyd had ever dared take with the dignified old Colonel. She emphasized each sentence with a gentle pull and pinch.

"Maybe you wouldn't believe it, but this little Mary Ware who is coming, has a most exalted opinion of me. From what Joyce says she thinks

I am perfect, and I don't want her disillusioned. It's so nice to have somebody look up to you that way, so I want to impress it on you that you're not to indulge in any reminiscence of my past while she is heah. You mustn't tell any of my youthful misdemeanahs that you are fond of telling — how I threw mud on yoah coat, in one of my awful tempahs, and smashed yoah shaving-mug with a walking-stick, and locked Walkah down in the coal cellah when he wouldn't do what I wanted him to. You must ' let the dead past bury its dead, and act — act in the living present,' so that she'll think that *you* think that I'm the piece of perfection she imagines me to be."

" I'll be a party to no such deception," answered the old Colonel, sternly, although his eyes, smiling fondly on her, plainly spoke consent. " You know you're the worst spoiled child in Oldham County."

" Whose fault is it? " retorted Lloyd, with a final pinch as she liberated his ears and darted away. " Ask Colonel George Lloyd. If there was any spoiling done, he did it."

Two hours later, still in the gayest of spirits, Lloyd and Betty raced down the avenue to meet their guests, and tired and travel-stained as the newcomers were, the impetuous greeting gave them a sense of having been caught up into a gay whirl of some kind. It gave them an excited thrill which presaged all sorts of delightful things about to happen. The courtly bows of the old Colonel, standing between the great white pillars, Mrs. Sherman's warm welcome, and Mom Beck's old-time curtseys, seemed to usher them into a fascinating story-book sort of life, far more interesting than any Mary had yet read.

Several hours later, sitting in the long drawing-room, she wondered if she could be the same girl who one short week before was chasing across the desert like a Comanche Indian, beating the bushes for rattlesnakes, or washing dishes in the hot little kitchen of the Wigwam. Here in the soft light shed from many waxen tapers in the silver candelabra, surrounded by fine old ancestral portraits, and furniture that shone with the polish of hospitable generations, Mary felt civilized down to her very finger-tips: so thoroughly a lady, through and through, that the sensation sent a warm thrill over her.

That feeling had begun soon after her arrival, when Mom Beck ushered her into a luxurious bathroom. Mary enjoyed luxury like a cat. As she splashed away in the big porcelain tub, she

wished that Hazel Lee could see the tiled walls,
the fine ample towels with their embroidered mono-
grams, the dainty soaps, and the cut-glass bottles of
toilet-water, with their faint odor as of distant
violets. Then she wondered if Mom Beck would
think that she had refused her offers of assistance
because she was not used to the services of a lady's
maid. She was half-afraid of this old family serv-
ant in her imposing head-handkerchief and white
apron.

Recalling Joyce's experiences in France and what
had been the duties of her maid, Marie, she decided
to call her in presently to brush her hair and tie
her slippers. Afterward she was glad that she had
done so, for Mom Beck was a practised hair-dresser,
and made the most of Mary's thin locks. She so
brushed and fluffed and be-ribboned them in a new
way, with a big black bow on top, that Mary
beamed with satisfaction when she looked in the
glass. The new way was immensely becoming.

Then when she went down to dinner, it seemed
so elegant to find Mr. Sherman in a dress suit. The
shaded candles and cut glass and silver and roses
on the table made it seem quite like the dinner-par-
ties she had read about in novels, and the talk that
circled around of the latest books and the new

opera, and the happenings in the world at large, and the familiar mention of famous names, made her feel as if she were in the real social whirl at last.

The name of copy-cat which Holland had given her proved well-earned now, for so easily did she fall in with the ways about her, that one would have thought her always accustomed to formal dinners, with a deft colored waiter like Alec at her elbow.

Rob dined with them, and later in the evening Mrs. Walton came strolling over in neighborly fashion, bringing her house-party to call on the other party, she said, though to be sure only half of her guests had arrived, the two young army officers, George Logan and Robert Stanley. Allison and Kitty were with them, and — Mary noted with a quick indrawn breath — *Ranald*. The title of *Little* Captain no longer fitted him. He was far too tall. She was disappointed to find him grown.

Somehow all the heroes and heroines whom she had looked upon as her own age, who *were* her own age when the interesting things she knew about them had happened, were all grown up. Her first disappointment had been in Rob, then in Betty. For this Betty was not the one Joyce had pictured in her stories of the first house-party. This one had long dresses, and her curly hair was tucked up on her head in such a bewitchingly young-ladified way that Mary was in awe of her at first. She was not disappointed in her now, however, and no longer in awe, since Betty had piloted her over the place, swinging hands with her in as friendly a fashion as if she were no older than Hazel Lee, and telling the way she looked when *she* saw The Locusts for the first time — a timid little country girl in a sunbonnet, with a wicker basket on her arm.

The military uniforms lent an air of distinction to the scene, and Allison and Kitty each began a conversation in such a vivacious way, that Mary found it difficult to decide which group to attach herself to. She did not want to lose a word that any one was saying, and the effort to listen to several separate conversations was as much of a strain as trying to watch three rings at the circus.

Through the laughter and the repartee of the young people she heard Mrs. Walton say to Mr. Sherman: " Yes, only second lieutenants, but I've been an army woman long enough to appreciate them as they deserve. They have no rank to speak of, few privileges, are always expected to do the agreeable to visitors (and they do it), obliged to give up their quarters at a moment's notice, take the duties nobody else wants, be cheerful under all conditions, and ready for anything. It is an exception when a second lieutenant is not dear and fascinating. As for these two, I am doubly fond of them, for their fathers were army men before them, and old-time friends of ours. George I knew as a little lad in Washington. I must tell you of an adventure of his, that shows what a sterling fellow he is."

Mary heard only part of the anecdote, for at the same time Kitty was telling an uproariously funny joke on Ranald, and all the rest were laughing. But she heard enough to make her take a second look at Lieutenant Logan. He was leaning forward in his chair, talking to Joyce with an air of flattering interest. And Joyce, in one of her new dresses, her face flushed a little from the unusual excitement, was talking her best and looking her prettiest.

" She's having a good time just like other girls," thought Mary, thankfully. " This will make up for lots of lonely times in the desert, when she was homesick for the high-school girls and boys at Plainsville. It would be fine if things would turn out so that Joyce liked an army man. If she married one and lived at a post she'd invite me to visit

"HE WAS LEANING FORWARD IN HIS CHAIR, TALKING TO
JOYCE"

her. Lieutenant Logan might be a general some
day, and it would be nice to have a great man in the
family. I wish mamma and Jack and Holland
could see what a good time we are having."

It did not occur to Mary that, curled up in a big
chair in the corner, she was taking no more active
share in the good times than the portraits on the
wall. Her eager smile and the alert happy look in
her eyes showed that she was all atingle with the
unusual pleasure the evening was affording her.
She laughed and looked and listened, sure that the
scene she was enjoying was as good as a play. She
had never seen a play, it is true; but she had read of
them, and of player folk, until she knew she was
fitted to judge of such things.

It was a pleasure just to watch the gleam of the
soft candle-light on Kitty's red ribbons, or on the
string of gold beads around Allison's white throat.
Maybe it was the candle-light which threw such a
soft glamour over everything and made it seem that
the pretty girls and the young lieutenants were only
portraits out of a beautiful old past who had stepped
down from their frames for a little while. Yet
when Mary glanced up, the soldier boy was still in
his picture on the wall, and the beautiful girl with
the June rose in her hair was still in her frame,

standing beside her harp, her white hand resting **on** its shining strings.

" It is my grandmothah Amanthis," explained Lloyd in answer to the lieutenant's question, as his gaze also rested admiringly on it. " Yes, this is the same harp you see in the painting. Yes, I play a little. I learned to please grandfathah."

Then, a moment later, Mary reached the **crown** of her evening's enjoyment, for Lloyd, in response to many voices, took her place beside the harp below the picture, and struck a few deep, rich chords. Then, with an airy running accompaniment, she began the Dove Song from the play of " The Princess Winsome: "

> " Flutter and fly, flutter and fly,
> Bear him my heart of gold."

It was all as Mary had imagined it would **be, a** hundred times in her day-dreams, only far sweeter and more beautiful. She had not thought how the white sleeves would fall back from the round white arms, or how her voice would go fluttering up like a bird, sweet and crystal clear on the last high note.

Afterward, when the guests were gone and everybody had said good night, Mary lay awake in the pink blossom of a room which she shared with

Joyce, the same room Joyce had had at the first house-party. She was having another good time, thinking it all over. She thought scornfully of the woman on the sleeping-car who had told her that distance lends enchantment, and that she must not expect too much of her promised land. She hoped she might meet that woman again some day, so that she could tell her that it was not only as nice as she had expected to find it, but a hundred times nicer.

She reminded herself that she must tell Betty about her in the morning. As she recalled one pleasant incident after another, she thought, " Now *this* is *life!* No wonder Lloyd is so bright and interesting when she has been brought up in such an atmosphere."

CHAPTER VI.

THE FOX AND THE STORK

LLOYD SHERMAN at seventeen was a combination of all the characters her many nicknames implied. The same imperious little ways and hasty outbursts of temper that had won her the title of Little Colonel showed themselves at times. But she was growing so much like the gentle maiden of the portrait that the name "Amanthis" trembled on the old Colonel's lips very often when he looked at her. The Tusitala ring on her finger showed that she still kept in mind the Road of the Loving Heart, which she was trying to leave behind her in every one's memory, and the string of tiny Roman pearls she sometimes clasped around her throat bore silent witness to her effort to live up to the story of Ederyn, and keep tryst with all that was expected of her.

When a long line of blue-blooded ancestors has handed down a heritage of proud traditions and family standards, it is no easy matter to be all that is expected of an only child. But Lloyd was meeting all expectations, responding to the influence of beauty and culture with which she had always been surrounded, as unconsciously as a bud unfolds to the sunshine. Her ambition " to make undying music in the world," to follow in the footsteps of her beautiful grandmother Amanthis, was in itself a reaching-up to one of the family ideals.

When the girls began calling her the Princess Winsome, unconsciously she began to reach up to be worthy of that title also, but when she found that Mary Ware was taking her as a model Maid of Honor, in all that that title implies, she began to feel that a burden was laid upon her shoulders. She had had such admirers before: little Magnolia Budine at Lloydsboro Seminary, and Cornie Dean at Warwick Hall. It was pleasant to know that they considered her perfection, but it was a strain to feel that she was their model, and that they copied her in everything, her faults as well as her graces. They had followed her like shadows, and such devotion grows tiresome.

Happily for Mary Ware, whatever else she did, she never bored any one. She was too independent and original for that. When she found an occasion to talk, she made the most of her opportunity, and talked with all her might, but her sensitiveness to surroundings always told her when it was time to retire into the background, and she could be so dumb as to utterly efface herself when the time came for her to keep silent.

A long list of delights filled her first letter home, but the one most heavily underscored, and chief among them all, was the fact that the big girls did not seem to consider her a " little pitcher " or a " tag." No matter where they went or what they talked about, she was free to follow and to listen. It was interesting to the verge of distraction when they talked merely of Warwick Hall and the school-girls, or recalled various things that had happened at the first house-party. But when they discussed the approaching wedding, the guests, the gifts, the decorations, and the feast, she almost held her breath in her eager enjoyment of it.

Several times a day, after the passing of the trains, Alec came up from the station with express packages. Most of them were wedding presents, which the bridesmaids pounced upon and carried away to the green room to await Eugenia's arrival. Every package was the occasion of much guessing and pinching and wondering, and the mystery was almost as exciting as the opening would have been.

The conversation often led into by-paths that were unexplored regions to the small listener in the background among the window-seat cushions: husbands and lovers and engagements, all the thrilling topics that a wedding in the family naturally suggests. Sometimes a whole morning would go by without her uttering a word, and Mrs. Sherman, who had heard what a talkative child she was, noticed her silence. Thinking it was probably dull for her, she reproached herself for not having provided some especial company for the entertainment of her youngest guest, and straightway set to work to do so.

Next morning a box of pink slippers was sent out from Louisville on approval, and the bridesmaids and maid of honor, seated on the floor in Betty's room, tried to make up their minds which to choose, — the kid or the satin ones. With each slim right foot shod in a fairy-like covering of shimmering satin, and each left one in daintiest pink kid, the three girls found it impossible to determine which was the prettier, and called upon Mary for her opinion.

All in a flutter of importance, she was surveying

the pretty exhibit of outstretched feet, when Mom Beck appeared at the door with a message from Mrs. Sherman. There was a guest for Miss Mary in the library. Would she please go down at once. Her curiosity was almost as great as her reluctance to leave such an interesting scene. She stood in the middle of the floor, wringing her hands.

" Oh, if I could only be in two places at once! " she exclaimed. " But maybe whoever it is won't stay long, and I can get back before you decide."

Hurrying down the stairs, she went into the library, where Mrs. Sherman was waiting for her.

" This is one of our little neighbors, Mary," she said, " Girlie Dinsmore."

A small-featured child of twelve, with pale blue eyes and long, pale flaxen curls, came forward to meet her. To Mary's horror, she held a doll in her arms almost as large as herself, and on the table beside her stood a huge toy trunk.

" I brought all of Evangeline's clothes with me," announced Girlie, as soon as Mrs. Sherman had left them to themselves. " 'Cause I came to stay all morning, and I knew she'd have plenty of time to wear every dress she owns."

Mary could not help the gasp of dismay that escaped her, thinking of that fascinating row of

pink slippers awaiting her up-stairs. From bridesmaids to doll-babies is a woful fall.

"Where is your doll?" demanded Girlie.

"Oh, I haven't any," said Mary, with a grown-up
shrug of the shoulders. "I stopped playing with
them ages ago."

Then realizing what an impolite speech that was,
she hastened to make amends by adding: "I sometimes dress Hazel Lee's, though. Hazel is one of
my friends back in Arizona. Once I made a whole
Indian costume for it like the squaws make. The
moccasins were made out of the top of a kid glove,
and beaded just like real ones."

Girlie's pale eyes opened so wide at the mention
of Indians that Mary almost forgot her disappointment at being called away from the big girls, and
proceeded to make them open still wider with her
tales of life on the desert. In a few moments she
carried the trunk out on to a vine-covered side
porch, where they made a wigwam out of two
hammocks and a sunshade, and changed the waxen
Evangeline into a blanketed squaw, with feathers
in her blond Parisian hair.

Mom Beck looked out several times, and finally
brought them a set of Lloyd's old doll dishes and
the daintiest of luncheons to spread on a low table.

There were olive sandwiches, frosted cakes, berries and cream, and bonbons and nuts in a silver dish shaped like a calla-lily.

For the first two hours Mary really enjoyed being hostess, although now and then she wished she could slip up-stairs long enough to see what the girls were doing. But when she had told all the interesting tales she could think of, cleared away the remains of the feast, and played with the doll until she was sick of the sight of it, she began to be heartily tired of Girlie's companionship.

"She's such a baby," she said to herself, impatiently. "She doesn't know much more than a kitten." It seemed to her that the third long hour never would drag to an end. But Girlie evidently enjoyed it. When the carriage came to take her home, she said, enthusiastically:

"I've had such a good time this morning that I'm coming over every single day while you're here. I can't ask you over to our house 'cause my grandma is so sick it wouldn't be any fun. We just have to tiptoe around and not laugh out loud. But I don't mind doing all the visiting."

"Oh, it will spoil everything!" groaned Mary to herself, as she ran up-stairs when Girlie was at last out of sight. She felt that nothing could compensate her for the loss of the whole morning, and the thought of losing any more precious time in that way was unendurable.

Mrs. Sherman met her in the hall, and pinched her cheek playfully as she passed her. " You make a charming little hostess, my dear," she said. " I looked out several times, and you were so absorbed with your play that it made me wish that I could be a little girl again, and join you with my poor old Nancy Blanche doll and my grand Amanthis that papa brought me from New Orleans. I'll have to resurrect them for you out of the attic, for I'm afraid it has been stupid for you here, with nobody your own age."

" Oh, no'm! Don't! Please don't!" protested Mary, a worried look on her honest little face. She was about to add, " I can't bear dolls any more. I only played with them to please Girlie," when Lloyd came out of her room with a letter.

" It's from the bride-to-be, mothah," she called, waving it gaily.

" She'll be heah day aftah to-morrow, so we can begin to put the finishing touches to her room. The day she comes I'm going to take the girls ovah to Rollington to get some long sprays of bride's wreath. Mrs. Crisp has two big bushes of it, white as snow. It will look so cool and lovely, everything in the room all green and white."

Mary stole away to her room, ready to cry. If every morning had to be spent with that tiresome Dinsmore child, she might as well have stayed on the desert.

"I simply have to get rid of her in some way," she mused. "It won't do to snub her, and I don't know any other way. I wish I could see Holland for about five minutes. He'd think of a plan."

So absorbed was she in her problem that she forgot to ask whether the kid or the satin slippers had been chosen, and she went down to lunch still revolving her trouble in her mind. On the dining-room wall opposite her place at table were two fine old engravings, illustrating the fable of the famous dinners given by the Fox and the Stork. In the first the stork strove vainly to fill its bill at the flat dish from which the fox lapped eagerly, while in the companion picture the fox sat by disconsolate while the stork dipped into the high slim pitcher, which the hungry guest could not reach.

Mary had noticed the pictures in a casual way every time she took a seat at the table, for the beast and the bird were old acquaintances. She had learned La Fontaine's version of the fable one time to recite at school. To-day, with the problem in her mind of how to rid herself of an unwelcome guest, they suddenly took on a new meaning.

" I'll do just the way the stork did," she thought, gleefully. " This morning Girlie had everything her way, and we played little silly baby games till I felt as flat as the dish that fox is eating out of. But she had a beautiful time. To-morrow morning I'm going to be stork, and make my conversation so deep she can't get her little baby mind into it at all. I'll be awfully polite, but I'll hunt up the longest words I can find in the dictionary, and talk about the books I've read, and she'll have such a stupid time she won't want to come again."

The course of action once settled upon, Mary fell to work with her usual energy. While the girls were taking their daily siesta, she dressed early and went down into the library. If it had not been for the fear of missing something, she would have spent much of her time in that attractive room. Books looked down so invitingly from the many shelves. All the June magazines lay on the library table, their pages still uncut. Everybody had been too busy to look at them. She hesitated a moment over the tempting array, but remembering her purpose, grimly passed them by and opened the big dictionary.

Rob found her still poring over it, pencil and paper in hand, when he looked into the room an hour later.

" What's up now? " he asked.

She evaded his question at first, but, afraid that he would tease her before the girls about her thirst for knowledge and her study of the dictionary, and that that might lead to the thwarting of her plans, she suddenly decided to take him into her confidence.

" Well," she began, solemnly, " you know mostly I loathe dolls. Sometimes I do dress Hazel Lee's for her, but I don't like to play with them regularly any more as I used to, — talk for them and all that. But Girlie Dinsmore was here this morning, and I had to do it because she is company. She had such a good time that she said she was coming over here every single morning while I'm here. I just can't have my lovely visit spoiled that way. The bride is coming day after to-morrow, and she'll be opening her presents and showing her trousseau to the girls, and I wouldn't miss it for anything. So I've made up my mind I'll be just as polite as possible. but I'll do as the stork did in the fable; make my entertainment so deep she won't enjoy it. I'm hunting up the longest words I can find and learning their definitions, so that I can use them properly."

Rob, looking over her shoulder, laughed to see the list she had chosen:

> " Indefatigability,
> Juxtaposition,
> Loquaciousness,
> Pabulum,
> Peregrinate,
> Longevous."

" You see," explained Mary, " sometimes there is a quotation after the word from some author, so I've copied a lot of them to use, instead of making up sentences myself. Here's one from Shakespeare about alacrity. And here's one from Arbuthnot, whoever he was, that will make her stare."

She traced the sentence with her forefinger, for Rob's glance to follow: *" Instances of longevity are chiefly among the abstemious."*

" Girlie won't have any more idea of what I'm talking about than a jay-bird."

To Mary's astonishment, the laugh with which Rob received her confidence was so long and loud it ended in a whoop of amusement, and when he had caught his breath he began again in such an infectious way that the girls up-stairs heard it and joined in. Then Lloyd leaned over the banister to call:

"What's the mattah, Rob? You all seem to be having a mighty funny time down there. Save your circus for us. We'll be down in a few minutes."

"This is just a little private side-show of Mary's and mine," answered Rob, going off into another peal of laughter at sight of Mary's solemn face. There was nothing funny in the situation to her whatsoever.

"Oh, don't tell, Mister Rob," she begged. "Please don't tell. Joyce might think it was impolite, and would put a stop to it. It seems funny to you, but when you think of my whole lovely visit spoiled that way — "

She stopped abruptly, so much in earnest that her voice broke and her eyes filled with tears.

Instantly Rob's laughter ceased, and he begged her pardon in such a grave, kind way, assuring her that her confidence should be respected, that her admiration of him went up several more degrees. When the girls came down, he could not be prevailed upon to tell them what had sent him off into such fits of laughter. "Just Mary's entertaining remarks," was all he would say, looking across at her with a meaning twinkle in his eyes. She immediately retired into the background as soon as the older girls appeared, but she sat admiring every word Rob said, and watching every movement.

"He's the very nicest man I ever saw," she said to herself. "He treats me as if I were grown up, and I really believe he likes to hear me talk."

Once when they were arranging for a tennis game for the next morning, he crossed the room with an amused smile, to say to her in a low aside: "I've thought of something to help along the stork's cause. Bring the little fox over to the tennis-court to watch the game. If she doesn't find that sufficiently stupid, and you run short of big words, read aloud to her, and tell her that is what you intend to do every day."

Such a pleased, gratified smile flashed over Mary's face that Betty exclaimed, curiously: "I certainly would like to know what mischief you two are planning. You laugh every time you look at each other."

Girlie Dinsmore arrived promptly next morning, trunk, doll, and all, expecting to plunge at once into an absorbing game of lady-come-to-see. But Mary

so impressed her with the honor that had been con-
ferred upon them by Mr. Moore's special invitation
to watch the tennis game that she was somewhat
bewildered.   She dutifully followed her resolute
hostess to the tennis-court, and took a seat beside
her with Evangeline clasped in her arms.   Neither
of the children had watched a game before, and
Girlie, not being able to understand a single move,
soon found it insufferably stupid.   But Mary be-
came more and more interested in watching a tall,
athletic figure in outing flannels and white shoes,
who swung his racket with the deftness of an ex-
pert, and who flashed an amused smile at her over
the net occasionally, as if he understood the situation and was enjoying it with her.

Several times when Rob's playing brought him
near the seat where the two children sat, he went
into unaccountable roars of laughter, for which the
amazed girls scolded him soundly, when he refused
to explain.   One time was when he overheard a
scrap of conversation.   Girlie had suggested a return to the porch and the play-house, and Mary
responded, graciously:

" Oh, we did all that yesterday morning, and I
think that even in the matter of playing dolls one
ought to be abstemious.   Don't you?   You know

"A TALL, ATHLETIC FIGURE IN OUTING FLANNELS"

Arbuthnot says that 'instances of longevity are chiefly among the abstemious,' and I certainly want to be longevous."

A startled expression crept into Girlie's pale blue eyes, but she only sat back farther on the seat and tightened her clasp on Evangeline. The next time Rob sauntered within hearing distance, a discussion of literature was in progress, Mary was asking:

" Have you ever read ' Old Curiosity Shop? ' "

The flaxen curls shook slowly in the motion that betokened she had not.

" Nothing of Dickens or Scott or Irving or Cooper? "

Still the flaxen curls shook nothing but no.

" Then what have you read, may I ask? " The superior tone of Mary's question made it seem that she was twenty years older than the child at her side, instead of only two.

" I like the Dotty Dimple books," finally admitted Girlie. " Mamma read me all of them and several of the Prudy books, and I have read half of ' Flaxie Frizzle ' my own self."

" *Oh!* " exclaimed Mary, in a tone expressing enlightenment. " I *see!* Nothing but juvenile books! No wonder that, with such mental pabulum, you don't care for anything but dolls! Now when I was your age, I had read ' The Vicar of Wakefield ' and ' Pride and Prejudice ' and Leather-stocking Tales, and all sorts of things. Probably that is why I lost my taste for dolls so early. Wouldn't you like me to read to you awhile every morning ? "

The offer was graciousness itself, but it implied such a lack on Girlie's part that she felt vaguely uncomfortable. She sat digging the toe of her slipper against the leg of the bench.

" I don't know," she stammered finally. " Maybe I can't come often. It makes me wigglesome to sit still too long and listen."

" We might try it this morning to see how you like it," persisted Mary. " I brought a copy of Longfellow out from the house, and thought you might like to hear the poem of ' Evangeline,' as long as your doll is named that."

Rob heard no more, for the game called him to another part of the court, but Mary's plan was a success. When the Dinsmore carriage came, Girlie announced that she wouldn't be over the next day, and maybe not the one after that. She didn't know for sure when she could come.

Rob stayed to lunch. As he passed Mary on the steps, he stooped to the level of her ear to say in a laughing undertone: " Congratulations, Miss Stork. I see your plan worked grandly."

Elated by her success and the feeling of good-comradeship which this little secret with Rob gave her, Mary skipped up on to the porch, well pleased with herself. But the next instant there was a curious change in her feeling. Lloyd, tall and graceful in her becoming tennis suit, was standing on the steps taking leave of some of the players. With hospitable insistence she was urging them to stay to lunch, and there was something in the sweet graciousness of the young hostess that made Mary uncomfortable. She felt that she had been weighed in the balance and found wanting. The Princess never would have stooped to treat a guest as she had treated Girlie. Her standard of hospitality was too high to allow such a breach of hospitality.

Mary had carried her point, but she felt that if Lloyd knew how she had played stork, she would consider her ill-bred. The thought worried her for days.

CHAPTER VII.

THE COMING OF THE BRIDE

EARLY in the June morning Mary awoke, feeling as if it were Christmas or Fourth of July or some great gala occasion. She lay there a moment, trying to think what pleasant thing was about to happen. Then she remembered that it was the day on which the bride was to arrive. Not only that, — before the sun went down, the best man would be at The Locusts also.

She raised herself on her elbow to look at Joyce, in the white bed across from hers. She was sound asleep, so Mary snuggled down on her pillow again, and lay quite still. If Joyce had been awake, Mary would have begun a long conversation about Phil Tremont. Instead, she began recalling to herself the last time she had seen him. It was three years ago, down by the beehives, and she had had no idea he was going away until he came to the Wigwam to bid them all good-by. And Joyce and Lloyd were away, so he had left a message for them with her. She thought it queer then, and she had wondered many times since why his farewell to the girls should have been a message about the old gambling god, Alaka. She remembered every word of it, even the tones of his voice as he said: "Try to remember just these words, please, Mary. Tell them that '*Alaka has lost his precious turquoises, but he will win them back again some day.*' Can you remember to say just that?"

He must have thought she wasn't much more than a baby to repeat it so carefully to her several times, as if he were teaching her a lesson. Well, to be sure, she was only eleven then, and she had almost cried when she begged him not to go away, and insisted on knowing when he was coming back. He had looked away toward old Camelback Mountain with a strange, sorry look on his face as he answered:

"Not till I've learned your lesson — to be 'inflexible.' When I'm strong enough to keep stiff in the face of any temptation, then I'll come back, little Vicar." Then he had stooped and kissed her hastily on both cheeks, and started off down the road, with her watching him through a blur of tears, because it seemed that all the good times in the world had suddenly come to an end. Away down the road he had turned to look back and wave his hat, and she had caught up her white sunbonnet and swung it high by its one limp string.

Afterward, when she went back to the swing by the beehives, she recalled all the old stories she had ever heard of knights who went out into the world to seek their fortunes, and waved farewell to some ladye fair in her watch-tower. She felt, in a vague way, that she had been bidden farewell by a brave knight errant. Although she was burning with curiosity when she delivered the message about the turquoises and Alaka, and wondered why Lloyd and Joyce exchanged such meaning glances, something kept her from asking questions, and she had gone on wondering all these years what it meant, and why there was such a sorry look in his eyes when he gazed out toward the old Camelback Mountain. Now, in the wisdom of her fourteen years, she began to suspect what the trouble had been, and resolved to ask Joyce for the solution of the mystery.

Now that Phil was twenty years old and doing a man's work in the world, she supposed she ought to call him Mr. Tremont, or, at least, Mr. Phil. Probably in his travels, with all the important

things that a civil engineer has to think of, he had
forgotten her and the way he had romped with her
at the Wigwam, and how he had saved her life
the time the Indian chased her. Being the bridegroom's brother and best man at the wedding, he
would scarcely notice her. Or, if he did cast a
glance in her direction, she had grown so much
probably he never would recognize her. Still, if
he *should* remember her, she wanted to appear at
her best advantage, and she began considering
what was the best her wardrobe afforded.

She lay there some time trying to decide whether
she should be all in white when she met him,
or in the dress with the little sprigs of forget-me-
nots sprinkled over it. White was appropriate for
all occasions, still the forget-me-nots would be suggestive. Then she remembered her mother's remark about that shade of blue being a trying one
for her to wear. That recalled Mom Beck's pre-
scription for beautifying the complexion. Nothing, so the old colored woman declared, was so
good for one's face as washing it in dew before the
sun had touched the grass, at the same time repeating a hoodoo rhyme. Mary had been intending to
try it, but never could waken early enough.

Now it was only a little after five. Slipping out

of bed, she drew aside the curtain. Smoke was rising from the chimney down in the servants' quarters, and the sun was streaming red across the lawn. But over by the side of the house, in the shadow of Hero's monument, the dew lay sparkling like diamonds on the daisies and clover that bloomed there — the only place on the lawn where the sun had not yet touched.

Thrusting her bare feet into the little red Turkish slippers beside her bed, Mary caught up her kimono lying over a chair. It was a long, Oriental affair, Cousin Kate's Christmas gift; a mixture of gay colors and a pattern of Japanese fans, and so beautiful in Mary's eyes that she had often bemoaned the fact that she was not a Japanese lady so that she could wear the gorgeous garment in public. It seemed too beautiful to be wasted on the privacy of her room.

Fastening it together with three of Joyce's little gold pins, she stole down the stairway. Mom Beck was busy in the dining-room, and the doors and windows stood open. Stepping out of one of the long French windows that opened on the side porch, Mary ran across to the monument. It was a glorious June morning. The myriads of roses were doubly sweet with the dew in their hearts.

A Kentucky cardinal flashed across the lawn ahead of her, darting from one locust-tree to another like a bit of live flame.

The little red Turkish slippers chased lightly over the grass till they reached the shadow of the monument. Then stooping, Mary passed her hands over the daisies and clover, catching up the dewdrops in her pink palms, and rubbing them over her face as she repeated Mom Beck's charm:

> " Beauty come, freckles go!
> Dewdops, make me white as snow! "

The dew on her face felt so cool and fresh that she tried it again, then several times more. Then she stooped over farther and buried her face in the wet grass, repeating the rhyme again with her eyes shut and in the singsong chant in which she often intoned things, without giving heed to what she was uttering. Suddenly, in the midst of this joyful abandon, an amused exclamation made her lift her head a little and open her eyes.

" By all the powers! What are you up to now, Miss Stork? "

Mary's head came up out of the wet grass with a jerk. Then her face burned an embarrassed crimson, for striding along the path toward her was Bob Moore, cutting across lots from Oaklea. He was bareheaded, and swinging along as if it were a pleasure merely to be alive on such a morning.

She sprang to her feet, so mortified at being caught in this secret quest for beauty that her embarrassment left her speechless. Then, remembering the way she was dressed, she sank down on the grass again, and pulled her kimono as far as possible over the little bare feet in the red slippers.

There was no need for her to answer his question. The rhyme she had been chanting was sufficient explanation.

" I thought you said," he began, teasingly, " that you were to have *your* innings when you were a grandmother; that you didn't care for beauty now if you could have a face like a benediction then."

" Oh, I didn't say that I didn't care! " cried Mary, crouching closer against the monument, and putting her arm across her face to hide it. " It's because I care so much that I'm always doing silly things and getting caught. I just wish the earth could open and swallow me! " she wailed.

Her head was bowed now till it was resting on her knees. Rob looked down on the little bunch of misery in the gay kimono, thinking he had never seen such a picture of woe. He could not help smiling, but he felt mean at having been the cause of her distress, and tried to think of something comforting to say.

"Sakes alive, child! That's nothing to feel bad about. Bathing your face in May-day dew is an old English custom that the prettiest girls in the Kingdom used to follow. I ought to apologize for intruding, but I didn't suppose any one was up. I just came over to say that some business for grandfather will take me to town on the earliest train, so that I can't be on hand when the best man arrives. I didn't want to wake up the entire household by telephoning, so I thought I'd step over and leave a message with Alec or some of them. If you'll tell Lloyd, I'll be much obliged."

"All right, I'll tell her," answered Mary, in muffled tones, without raising her head from her knees. She was battling back the tears, and felt that she could never face the world again. She waited till she was sure Rob was out of sight, and then, springing up, ran for the shelter of her room. As she stole up the stairs, her eyes were so blinded with tears that she could hardly see the steps; tears of humiliation, that Rob, of all people, whose good opinion she valued, should have discovered her in a situation that made her appear silly and vain.

Luckily for the child's peace of mind, Betty had also wakened early that morning, and was taking advantage of the quiet hours before breakfast to attend to her letter-writing. Through her open door she caught sight of the woebegone little figure slipping past, and the next instant Mary found herself in the white and gold room with Betty's arm around her, and her tearful face pressed against a sympathetic shoulder. Little by little Betty coaxed from her the cause of her tears, then sat silent, patting her hand, as she wondered what she could say to console her.

To the older girl it seemed a matter to smile over, and the corners of her mouth did dimple a little, until she realized that to Mary's supersensitive nature this was no trifle, and that she was suffering keenly from it.

" Oh, I'm so ashamed," sobbed Mary. " I never want to look Mister Rob in the face again. I'd rather go home and miss the wedding than meet him any more."

" Nonsense," said Betty, lightly. " Now you're making a mountain out of a mole-hill. Probably Rob will never give the matter a second thought, and he would be amazed if he thought you did. I've heard you say you wished you could be just like Lloyd. Do you know, her greatest charm to me is that she never seems to think of the impression she is making on other people. Now, if she should decide that her complexion would be better for a wash in the dew, she would go ahead and wash it, no matter who caught her at it, and, first thing you know, all the Valley would be following her example.

"I'm going to preach you a little sermon now, because I've found out your one fault. It isn't very big yet, but, if you don't nip it in the bud, it will be like Meddlesome Matty's, —

> "'Which, like a cloud before the skies,
> Hid all her better qualities.'

"You are self-conscious, Mary. Always thinking about the impression you are making on people, and so eager to please that it makes you miserable if you think you fall short of any of their standards. I knew a girl at school who let her sensitiveness to other people's opinions run away with her. She was so anxious for her friends to be pleased with her that she couldn't be natural. If anybody glanced in the direction of her head, she immediately began to fix her side-combs, or if they seemed to be noticing her dress, she felt her belt and looked down at herself to see if anything was wrong. Half the time they were not looking at her at all, and not even giving her a thought. And I've known her to agonize for days over some trifle, some remark she had made or some one had made to her, that every one but her had forgotten. She developed into a dreadful bore, because she never could forget herself, and was always looking at her affairs through a magnifying-glass.

"Now if you should keep out of Rob's way after this, and act as if you had done something to be ashamed of, which you have not, don't you see that your very actions would remind him of what you want him to forget? But if when you meet him you are your own bright, cheerful, friendly little self, this morning's scene will fade into a dim background."

Only half-convinced, Mary nodded that she understood, but still proceeded to wipe her eyes at intervals.

"Then, there's another thing," continued Betty. "If you sit and brood over your mortification, it will spread all over your sky like a black cloud, till it will seem bigger than any of the good times

you have had. In the dear old garden at Warwick
Hall there is a sun-dial that has this inscription on
it, ' I only mark the hours that shine.' So I am
going to give you that as a text. Now, dear, that is
the end of my sermon, but here is the application."

She pointed to a row of little white books on the
shelf above her desk, all bound in kid, with her
initials stamped on the back in gold. " Those are
my good-times books. ' I only mark the hours that
shine' in them, and when things go wrong and
I get discouraged over my mistakes, I glance
through them and find that there's lots more to
laugh over than cry about, and I'm going to recom-
mend the same course to you. Godmother gave
me the first volume when I came to the first house-
party, and the little record gave me so much pleasure that I've gone on adding volume after volume.
Suppose you try it, dear. Will you, if I give you
a book?"

" Yes," answered Mary, who had heard of these
books before, and longed for a peep into them.
She had her wish now, for, taking them down
from the shelf, Betty read an extract here and there,
to illustrate what she meant. Presently, to their
astonishment, they heard Mom Beck knocking at
Lloyd's door to awaken her, and Betty realized with

a start that she had been reading over an hour. Her letters were unanswered, but she had accomplished something better. Mary's tears had dried, as she listened to these accounts of their frolics at boarding-school and their adventures abroad, and in her interest in them her own affairs had taken their proper proportion. She was no longer heart-broken over having been discovered by Rob, and she was determined to overcome the sensitiveness and self-consciousness which Betty had pointed out as her great fault.

As she rose to go, Betty opened a drawer in her desk and took out a square, fat diary, bound in red morocco. " One of the girls gave me this last Christmas," she said. " I never have used it, because I want to keep my journals uniform in size and binding, and I'll be so glad to have you take it and start a record of your own, if you will."

" Oh, I'll begin this very morning! " cried Mary, in delight, throwing her arms around Betty's neck with an impulsive kiss, and trying to express her thanks.

" Then wait till I write my text in it," said Betty, " so that it will always recall my sermon. I've talked to you as if I were your grandmother, haven't I ? "

" You've made me feel a lot more comfortable,"
answered Mary, humbly, with another kiss as Betty
handed her the book. On the fly-leaf she had written her own name and Mary's and the inscription
borne by the old sun-dial in Warwick Hall garden:

" I only mark the hours that shine."

It was after lunch before Mary found a moment
in which to begin her record, and then it was in
unconscious imitation of Betty's style that she wrote
the events of the morning. Probably she would
not have gone into details and copied whole conversations if she had not heard the extracts from
Betty's diaries. Betty was writing for practice as
well as with the purpose of storing away pleasant
memories, so it was often with the spirit of the
novelist that she made her entries.

" It seems hopeless to go back to the beginning,"
wrote Mary, " and tell all that has happened so far,
so I shall begin with this morning. Soon after
breakfast we went to Rollington in the carriage,
Joyce and Betty and I on the back seat, and Lloyd
in front with the coachman. And Mrs. Crisp cut
down nearly a whole bushful of bridal wreath to
decorate Eugenia's room with. When we got back
May Lily had just finished putting up fresh cur-

tains in the room, almost as fine and thin as frost-work. The furniture is all white, and the walls a soft, cool green, and the rugs like that dark vel-vety moss that grows in the deepest woods. When we had finished filling the vases and jardinières, the room itself all snowy white and green made you think of a bush of bridal wreath.

"We were barely through with that when it was time for Lloyd and Aunt Elizabeth to go to the station to meet Eugenia. There wasn't room for the rest of us in the carriage, so Betty and Joyce and I hung out of the windows and watched for them, and Betty and Joyce talked about the other time Eugenia came, when they walked up and down under the locusts waiting for her and wondering what she would be like. When she did come, they were half-afraid of her, she was so stylish and young-ladified, and ordered her maid about in such a superior way.

"Betty said it was curious how snippy girls of that age can be sometimes, and then turn out to be such fine women afterward, when they outgrow their snippiness and snobbishness. Then she told us a lot we had never heard about the school Eu-genia went to in Germany to take a training in housekeeping, and so many interesting things about her that I was all in a quiver of curiosity to see her.

"When we heard the carriage coming, Betty and Joyce tore down-stairs to meet her, but I just hung farther out of the window. And, oh, but she was pretty and stylish and tall — and just as Betty had said, *patrician*-looking, with her dusky hair and big dark eyes. She is the Spanish type of beauty. She swept into the house so grandly, with her maid following with her satchels (the same old Eliot who was here before), that I thought for a moment maybe she was as stuck-up as ever. But when she saw her old room, she acted just like a happy little girl, ready to cry and laugh in the same breath because everything had been made so beautiful for her coming. While she was still in the midst of admiring everything, she sat right down on the bed and tore off her gloves, so that she could open the queer-looking parcel she carried. I had thought maybe it was something too valuable to put in the satchels, but it was only a new kind of egg-beater she had seen in a show-window on her way from one depot to another. You would have thought from the way she carried on that she had found a wonderful treasure. And in the midst of showing us that she exclaimed:

" ' Oh, girls, what do you think? I met the dear-est old lady on the sleeper, and she gave me a receipt for a new kind of salad. That makes ten kinds of salad that I know how to make. Oh, I just can't wait to tell you about our little love of a house! It's all furnished and waiting for us. Papa and I were out to look all over it the day I started, and everything was in place but the refrigerator, and Stuart had already ordered one sent out.'

" Then Lloyd opened the closet door and called her attention to the great pile of packages waiting to be opened. She flew at them and called us all to help, and for a little while Mom Beck and Eliot were kept busy picking up strings and wrapping-paper and cotton and excelsior. When we were through, the bed and the chairs and mantel and two extra tables that had been brought in were piled with the most beautiful things I ever saw. I never dreamed there were such lovely things in the world as some of the beaten silver and hand-painted china and Tiffany glass. There was a jew-elled fan, and all sorts of things in gold and mother-of-pearl, and there was some point lace that she said was more suitable for a queen than a young

American girl. Her father has so many wealthy friends, and they all sent presents.

" Opening the bundles was so much fun, — like a continual surprise-party, Betty said, or a hundred Christmases rolled into one. Between times when Eugenia wasn't exclaiming over how lovely everything was, she was telling us how the house was furnished, and what a splendid fellow Stuart is, and how wild she is for us to know him. I had never heard a bride talk before, and she was so *happy* that somehow it made you feel that getting married was the most beautiful thing in the world.

" One of the first things she did when she opened her suit-case was to take out a picture of Stuart. It was a miniature on ivory in a locket of Venetian gold, because it was in Venice he had proposed to her. After she had shown it to us, she put it in the centre of her dressing-table, with the white flowers all around it, as if it had been some sort of shrine. There was a look in her eyes that made me think of the picture in Betty's room of a nun laying lilies on an altar.

" It is after luncheon now, and she has gone to her room to rest awhile. So have the other girls. But I couldn't sleep. The days are slipping by too fast for me to waste any time that way."

The house was quiet when Mary closed her journal. Joyce was still asleep on the bed, and through the open door she could see Betty, tilted back in a big chair, nodding over a magazine. She concluded it would be a good time to dash off a letter to Holland, but with a foresight which prompted her to be ready for any occasion, she decided to dress first for the evening. Tiptoeing around the room, she brushed her hair in the new way Mom Beck had taught her, and, taking out her prettiest white dress, proceeded to array herself in honor of the best man's coming. Then she rummaged in the tray of her trunk till she found her pink coral necklace and fan-chain, and, with a sigh of satisfaction that she was ready for any emergency, seated herself at her letter-writing.

She had written only a page, however, when the clock on the stairs chimed four. The deep tones echoing through the hall sent Lloyd bouncing up from her couch, her hair falling over her shoulders and her long kimono tripping her at every step, as she ran into Joyce's room.

"What are we going to do?" she cried in dismay. "I ovahslept myself, and now it's foah o'clock, and Phil's train due in nine minutes. The carriage is at the doah and none of us dressed to go to meet him. I wrote that the entiah bridal party would be there."

Joyce sprang up in a dazed sort of way, and began putting on her slippers. The bridesmaids had talked so much about the grand welcome the best man was to receive on his entrance to the Valley that, half-awake as she was, she could not realize that it was too late to carry out their plans.

"Oh, it's no use trying to get ready now," said Lloyd, in a disappointed tone. "We couldn't dress and get to the station in time to save ou' lives." Then her glance fell on Mary, sitting at her desk in all her brave array of pink ribbons and corals.

"Why, Mary can go!" she cried, in a relieved tone. "I had forgotten that she knows Phil as well as we do. Run on, that's a deah! Don't stop for a hat! You won't need it in the carriage. Tell him that you're the maid of honah on this occasion!"

It was all over so quickly, the rapid drive down the avenue, the quick dash up to the station as the train came puffing past, that Mary had little time to rehearse the part she had been bidden to play. She was so afraid that Phil would not recognize her that she wondered if she ought not to begin by introducing herself. She pictured the scene in her mind as they rolled along, unconscious that she was smiling and bowing into empty air, as she rehearsed the speech with which she intended to impress him. She would be as dignified and gracious as the Princess herself; not at all like the hoydenish child of eleven who had waved her sunbonnet at him in parting three years before.

The sight of the train as it slowed up sent a queer inward quiver of expectancy through her, and her cheeks were flushed with eagerness as she leaned forward watching for him. With a nervous gesture, she put her hand up to her hair-ribbons to make sure that her bows were in place, and then clutched the coral necklace. Then Betty's sermon flashed across her mind, and the thought that she had done just like the self-conscious girl at school brought a distressed pucker between her eyebrows. But the next instant she forgot all about it. She forgot the princess-like way in which she was to step from the carriage, the dignity with which she was to offer Phil her hand, and the words wherewith she was to welcome him. She had caught sight of a wide-brimmed gray hat over the heads of the crowd, and a face, bronzed and handsome, almost as dear in its familiar outlines as Jack's or Holland's. Her carefully rehearsed actions flew to the winds, as, regardless of the strangers all about, she sprang from the carriage and ran along bareheaded in the sun. And Phil, glancing around him for the bridal party that was to meet him, was surprised beyond measure when this little apparition from the Arizona Wigwam caught him by the hand.

" Bless my soul, it's the little Vicar!" he exclaimed. " Why, it's like getting back home to see *you!* And how you've grown, and how really civilized you are!"

So he *had* remembered her. He was glad to see her. With her face glowing and her feet fairly dancing, she led him to the carriage, pouring out a flood of information as they went, about The Locusts and the wedding and the people they passed, and how lovely everything was in the Valley, till he said, with a twinkle in his eyes: " You're the same enthusiastic little soul that you used to be, aren't you? I hope you'll speak as good a word for me at The Locusts as you did at Lee's ranch. I am taking it as a good omen that you were sent to conduct me into this happy land. You made a success of it that other time; somehow I'm sure you will this time."

All the way to the house Mary sat and beamed

on him as she talked, thinking how much older he looked, and yet how friendly and brotherly he still was. She introduced him to Mrs. Sherman with a proud, grandmotherly air of proprietorship, and took a personal pride in every complimentary thing said about him afterward, as if she were responsible for his good behavior, and was pleased with the way he was " showing off."

Rob came over as usual in the evening. Phil was not there at first. He and Eugenia were strolling about the grounds. Mary, sitting in a hammock on the porch, was impatient for them to come in, for she wanted to see what impression he would make on Rob, whom she had been thinking lately was the nicest man she ever met. She wanted to see them together to contrast the two, for they seemed wonderfully alike in size and general appearance. In actions, too, Mary thought, remembering how they both had teased her.

She had not seen Rob since their unhappy encounter early that morning, when she had been so overcome with mortification; and if Betty had not been on the porch also, she would have found it hard to stay and face him. But she wanted to show Betty that she had taken her little sermon to heart. Then, besides, the affair did not look so

big, after all that had happened during this exciting day.

As they waited, Joyce joined them, and presently
they heard Lloyd coming through the hall. She
was singing a verse from Ingelow's " Songs of
Seven : "

> " ' There is no dew left on the daisies and clover.
> There is no rain left in the heaven.
> I've said my seven times over and over —
> Seven times one are seven.' "

Then she began again, " ' There is no dew left
on the daisies and clover — ' " Rob turned to
Mary. " I wonder why," he said, meaningly.

The red flashed up into Mary's face and she made
no audible answer, but Joyce, turning suddenly,
saw to her horror that Mary had made a saucy
face at him and thrust out her tongue like a naughty
child.

" Why, Mary Ware ! " she began, in a shocked
tone, but Betty interrupted with a laugh. " Let
her alone, Joyce; he richly deserved it. He was
teasing her."

" Betty was right," thought Mary afterward.
" It *was* better to make fun of his teasing than to
run off and cry because he happened to mention

the subject. If I had done that, he never would have said to Betty afterward that I was the jolliest little thing that ever came over the pike. How much better this day has ended than it began."

CHAPTER VIII.

AT THE BEECHES

THE invitation came by telephone while the family was at breakfast next morning. Would the house-party at The Locusts join the house-party at The Beeches in giving a series, of tableaux at their lawn fête that night? If so, would the house-party at The Locusts proceed immediately to The Beeches to spend the morning in the rehearsing of tableaux, the selection of costumes, the manufacture of paper roses, and the pleasure of each other's honorable company in the partaking of a picnic-lunch under the trees?

There was an enthusiastic acceptance from all except Eugenia, who, tired from her long journey and with many important things to attend to, begged to be left behind for a quiet day with her cousin Elizabeth. Mary, tormented by a fear that maybe she was not included in the invitation, since she was a child, and all the guests at The Beeches were grown, could scarcely finish her breakfast in her excitement. But long before the girls were ready to start, her fears were set at rest by the arrival of Elise Walton in her pony-cart. She wanted Mary to drive to one of the neighbors with her, to borrow a bonnet and shawl over fifty years old, which were to figure in one of the tableaux.

Elise had not been attracted by Mary's appearance the day she met her in the restaurant and was not sure that she would care for her. It was only her hospitable desire to be nice to a guest in the Valley that made her comply so willingly to her mother's request to show her some especial attention. Mary, spoiled by the companionship of the older girls for the society of those her own age, was afraid that Elise would be a repetition of Girlie Dinsmore; but before they had gone half a mile together they were finding each other so vastly entertaining that by the time they reached The Beeches they felt like old friends.

It was Mary's first sight of the place, except the glimpse she had caught through the trees the morning they passed on their way to Rollington. As the pony-cart rattled up the wide carriage drive which swept around in front of the house, she felt as if she were riding straight into a beautiful old Southern story of ante-bellum days. Back into the times

when people had leisure to make hospitality their
chief business in life, and could afford for every
day to be a holiday.   When there were always
guests under the spreading rooftree of the great
house, and laughter and plenty in the servants'
quarters. The sound of a banjo and a negro melody
somewhere in the background heightened the effect
of that illusion.

The wide front porch seemed full of people.
Allison and Kitty looked up with a word of greeting as the two girls came up, one carrying the bonnet and the other the shawl, but nobody seemed to
think it necessary to introduce Elise's little friend
to the other guests. It would have been an embar-
rassing ordeal for her, for there were so many
strangers. Mary recognized the two young lieutenants.

With the help of a pretty brunette in white,
whom Elise whispered was Miss Bonham from
Lexington, they were rigging up some kind of a
coat of mail for Lieutenant Logan to wear in one
of the tableaux. Ranald, with a huge sheet of
cardboard and the library shears, was manufactur-
ing a pair of giant scissors, half as long as himself,
which a blonde in blue was waiting to cover with
tin foil. She was singing coon songs while she

waited, to the accompaniment of a mandolin, and in such a gay, rollicking way, that every one was keeping time either with hand or foot.

"That is Miss Bernice Howe," answered Elise, in response to Mary's whispered question. "She lives here in the Valley. And that's Malcolm MacIntyre, my cousin, who is sitting beside her. That's his brother Keith helping Aunt Allison with the programme cards."

Mary stared at the two young men, vaguely disappointed. They were the two little knights of Kentucky, but they were grown up, like all the other heroes and heroines she had looked forward to meeting. She told herself that she might have expected it, for she knew that Malcolm was Joyce's age; but she had associated them so long with the handsome little fellows in the photograph Lloyd had, clad in the knightly costumes of King Arthur's time, that it was hard to recognize them now, in these up-to-date, American college boys, who had long ago discarded their knightly disguises.

"And that," said Elise, as another young man came out of the house with a sheet of music in his hand for Miss Howe, "is Mister Alex Shelby. He lives in Louisville, but he comes out to the Valley all the time to see Bernice. I'll tell you about them while we drive over to Mrs. Bisbee's.

"It's this way," she began a few moments later, as they rattled down the road; " Bernice asked Allison if Mister Shelby couldn't be in one of the tableaux. Allison said yes, that they had intended to ask him before she spoke of it; that they had decided to ask him to be the boatman in the tableau of ' Elaine, the Lily Maid of Astolat.' But when Bernice found that Lloyd had already been asked to be Elaine, she was furious. She said she was just as good as engaged to him, or something of the sort, I don't know exactly what. And she knew, if Lloyd had a chance to monopolize him in that beautiful tableau, what it would lead to. It wouldn't be the first time that Lloyd had quietly stepped in and taken possession of her particular friends. She made such a fuss about it, that Allison finally said she'd change, and make Malcolm take the part of boatman, and give Alex the part they had intended for Malcolm, even if they didn't fit as well."

" The hateful thing!" sputtered Mary, indignantly. " I don't see how she can insinuate such mean things about any one as sweet and beautiful as Lloyd is."

" I don't either," agreed Elise, " but Allison says

it is true that everybody who has ever started out as a special friend of Bernice, men I mean, have ended by thinking the most of Lloyd. But everybody knows that it is simply because she is more attractive than Bernice. As Ranald says Lloyd isn't a girl to fish for attention, and that Bernice would have more if she didn't show the fellows that she was after them with a hook. Don't you tell Lloyd I told you all this," warned Elise.

" Oh, I wouldn't think of doing such a thing!" cried Mary. " It would hurt her dreadfully to know that anybody talked so mean about her. I wouldn't be the one to repeat it, for worlds!"

Left to hold the pony while Elise went in at Mrs. Bisbee's, Mary sat thinking of the snake she had discovered in her Eden. It was a rude shock to find that every one did not admire and love the " Queen of Hearts," who to her was without fault or flaw. All the rest of that day and evening, she could not look in Bernice Howe's direction, without a savage desire to scratch her. Once, when she heard her address Lloyd as " dearie," she could hardly keep from crying out, " Oh, you sly, two-faced creature!"

Lloyd and her guests arrived on the scene while Mary was away in the pony-cart on another borrowing expedition. All of the tableaux, except two, were simple in setting, requiring only the costumes that could be furnished by the chests of the neighborhood attics. But those two kept everybody busy all morning long. One was the reproduction of a famous painting called June, in which seven garlanded maidens in Greek costumes posed in a bewitching rose bower. Quantities of roses were needed for the background, great masses of them that would not fade and droop; and since previous experience had proved that artificial flowers may be used with fine stage effect in the glare of red footlights the whole place was bursting into tissue-paper bloom. The girls cut and folded the myriad petals needed, the boys wired them, and a couple of little pickaninnies sent out to gather foliage, piled armfuls of young oak-leaves on the porch to twine into long conventional garlands, like the ones in the painting.

Agnes Waring had come over to help with the Greek costumes, and since the long folds of cheesecloth could be held in place by girdles, basting threads, and pins, the gowns were rapidly finished.

Down by the tea-house the colored coachman sawed and pounded and planed under Malcolm's occasional direction. He was building a barge like

the one described in Tennyson's poem of the **Lily**
Maid of Astolat. From time to time, Lloyd, who
was to personate Elaine, was called to stretch herself out on the black bier in the centre, to see if it
was long enough or high enough or wide enough,
before the final nails were driven into place.

Malcolm, with a pole in his hand, posed as the
old dumb servitor who was to row her up the river.
It all looked unpromising enough in the broad daylight; the boat with its high stiff prow made of dry
goods boxes and covered with black calico, and
Lloyd stretched out on the bier in a modern shirt-
waist suit with side-combs in her hair. She gig-
gled as she meekly crossed her hands on her breast,
with a piece of newspaper folded in one to repre-
sent the letter, and a bunch of lilac leaves in the
other, which later was to clasp the lily. From under
the long eyelashes lying on her cheeks, she smiled
mischievously at Malcolm, who was vainly trying
to put a decrepit bend into his athletic young back,
as he bent over the pole in the attitude of an old,
old man.

"Yes, it does look silly now," admitted Miss
Allison in answer to his protest that he felt like a
fool. "But wait till you get on the long white
beard and wig I have for you, and the black robe.

You'll look like Methuselah. And Lloyd will be covered with a cloth of gold, and her hair will be rippling down all over her shoulders like gold, too. And we've a real lily for the occasion, a long stalk of them. Oh, this tableau is to be the gem of the collection."

"But half the people here won't understand it," said Malcolm.

"Yes, they will, for we're to have readings behind the scenes in explanation of each one. We've engaged an amateur elocutionist for the occasion. I'll show you just the part she'll read for this scene, so you'll know how long you have to pose to-night. It begins with those lines, 'And the dead, oared by the dumb, went upward with the flood. In her right hand the lily, in her left the letter.' Where did I put that volume of Tennyson?"

"Here it is," answered Mary Ware, unexpectedly, springing up from her seat on the grass to hand her the volume. She had been watching the rehearsal with wide-eyed interest. Deep down in her romance-loving little soul had long been the desire to see Sir Feal the Faithful face to face, and hear him address the Princess. The play of the "Rescue of the Princess Winsome" had become a real thing to her, that she felt that it must have happened; that Malcolm really was Lloyd's true knight, and that when they were alone together they talked like the people in books. She was disappointed when the rehearsal was over because the conversation she had imagined did not take place.

The coachman's carpenter-work was not of the steadiest, and Lloyd lay laughing on the shaky bier because she could not rise without fear of upsetting it.

" Help me up, you ancient mariner," she ordered, and when Malcolm, instead of springing forward in courtly fashion to her assistance as Sir Feal should have done, playfully held out his pole for her to pull herself up by, Mary felt that something was wrong. A playful manner was not seemly on the part of a Sir Feal. It would have been natural enough for Phil or Rob to do teasing things, but she resented it when there seemed a lack of deference on Malcolm's part toward the Princess.

After they had gone back to the porch, Mary sat on the grass a long time, reading the part of the poem relating to the tableau. She and Holland had committed to memory several pages of the " Idylls of the King," and had often run races repeating them, to see which could finish first. Now Mary found that she still remembered the entire page that Miss Allison had read. She closed the book, and repeated it to herself.

> " So that day there was dole in Astolat.
>
> .   .   .   .
>
> Then rose the dumb old servitor, and the dead,
> Oared by the dumb, went upward with the flood —
> In her right hand the lily, in her left
> The letter — all her bright hair streaming down —
> And all the coverlid was cloth of gold —
> Drawn to her waist, and she herself in white.
> All but her face, and that clear-featured face
> Was lovely, for she did not seem as dead,
> But fast asleep, and lay as though she smiled."

That was as far as Mary got with her whispered declamation, for two white-capped maids came out and began spreading small tables under the beech-tree where she sat. She opened the book and began reading, because she did not know what else to do. While she had been watching Lloyd in the boat, Elise had been summoned to the house to try on the dress she was to wear in the tableau of the gipsy fortune-teller. The people on the porch had divided into little groups which she did not feel free to join. She was afraid they would think she was intruding. Even her own sister seemed out of her reach, for she and Lieutenant Logan had taken their share of paper roses over to a rustic

seat near the croquet grounds and were talking
more busily than they were fashioning tissue
flowers.

Mary was unselfishly glad that Joyce was having
attention like the other girls and that she had been
chosen for one of the Greek maidens in the tableau
of June. And she wasn't really jealous of Elise
because she was to be tambourine girl in the gipsy
scene, but she did wish, with a little fluttering sigh,
that she could have had some small part in it all.
It was hard to be the only plain one in the midst of
so many pretty girls; so plain that nobody even
thought of suggesting her for one of the characters.

" I know very well," she said to herself, " that
a Lily Maid of Astolat with freckles would be ridiculous, and I'm not slim and graceful enough to be a
tambourine girl, but it would be so nice to have
some part in it. It would be such a comfortable
feeling to know that you're pretty enough always
to be counted in."

Her musings were interrupted by the descent of
the party upon the picnic tables, and she looked up
to see Elise beckoning her to a seat. To her delight
it was at the table opposite the one where Lloyd
and Phil, Anna Moore and Keith were seated.
Malcolm was just across from them, with Miss

Bonham on one side and Betty and Lieutenant Stanley on the other. Mary looked around inquiringly for her sister. She was with Rob now, and Lieutenant Logan was placing chairs for Allison and himself on the other side of the tree. Mr. Shelby and the hateful Miss Bernice Howe were over there, too, Mary noted, glad that they were at a distance.

Malcolm was still in a teasing mood, it seemed, for as Lloyd helped herself in picnic fashion from a plate of fried chicken, he said, laughing, "Look at Elaine now. Tennyson wouldn't know his Lily Maid if he saw her in this way." He struck an attitude, declaiming dramatically, "In her right hand the wish-bone, in her left the olive."

"That's all right," answered Lloyd, tossing the olive stone out on the grass, and helping herself to a beaten biscuit. "I always did think that Elaine was a dreadful goose to go floating down the rivah to a man who didn't care two straws about her. She'd much bettah have held on to a wish-bone and an olive and stayed up in her high towah with her fathah and brothahs who appreciated her. She would have had a bettah time and he would have had lots moah respect for her."

"Oh, I don't think so," cooed Miss Bonham,

with a coquettish side glance at Phil. " That always seemed such a beautifully romantic situation to me. Doesn't it appeal to you, Mr. Tremont?"

Mary listened for Phil's answer with grave attention, for she, too, considered it a touching situation, and more than once had pictured, in pleasing day-dream, herself as Elaine, floating down a stream in that poetic fashion.

" Well, no, Miss Bonham," said Phil, laughingly. " I'm free to confess that if I had been Sir Lancelot, I'd have liked her a great deal better if she had been a cheerful sort of body, and had stayed alive. Then if she had come rowing up in a nice trig little craft, instead of that spooky old funeral barge, and had offered me a wish-bone and an olive, I'd have thought them twice as fetching as a lily and that doleful letter. I'd have joined her picnic in a jiffy, and probably had such a jolly time that the poem would have ended with wedding bells in the high tower instead of a funeral dirge in the palace.

" She wasn't game," he continued, smiling across at Mary, who was listening with absorbing attention. " Now if she had only lived up to the Vicar of Wakefield's motto — instead of mooning over Lancelot's old shield, and embroidering things for

it, and acting as if it were something too precious
for ordinary mortals to touch — if she'd batted it
into the corner, or made mud pies on it, to show
that she was inflexible, fortune *would* have changed
in her favor. Sir Lancelot would have had some
respect for her common sense."

Mary, who felt that the remark was addressed
to her, crimsoned painfully. Rob took up the question, and his opinion was the same as Phil's and
Malcolm's. Long after the conversation passed to
other topics, Mary puzzled over the fact that the
three knightliest-looking men she knew, the three
who, she supposed, would make ideal lovers, had
laughed at one of the most romantic situations in
all poesy, and had agreed that Elaine was silly and
sentimental. Maybe, she thought with burning
cheeks, maybe they would think she was just as
bad if they knew how she had admired Elaine and
imagined herself in her place, and actually cried
over the poor maiden who loved so fondly and so
truly that she could die of a broken heart.

When she reflected that Lloyd, too, had agreed
with them, she began to think that her own ideals
might need reconstructing. She was glad that
Phil's smile had seemed to say that he took it for
granted that she would have been inflexible to the

extent of making mud pies on Lancelot's shield.
Unconsciously her reconstruction began then and
there, for although the seeds sown by the laughing discussion at the picnic table lay dormant
in her memory many years, they blossomed into a
saving common sense at last, that enabled her to see
the humorous side of the most sentimental situation, and gave her wisdom to meet it as it deserved.

The outdoor tableaux that night proved to be
one of the most successful entertainments ever given
in the Valley. A heavy wire, stretched from one
beech-tree to another, held the curtains that hid
the impromptu stage. The vine-covered tea-house
and a dense clump of shrubbery formed the background. Rows of Japanese lanterns strung from
the gate to the house, and from pillar to pillar of
the wide porches, gave a festive appearance to the
place, but they were not really needed. The full
moon flooded the lawn with a silvery radiance, and
as the curtains parted each time, a flash of red
lights illuminated the tableaux.

It was like a glimpse of fairy-land to Mary, and
she had the double enjoyment of watching the arrangement of each group behind the scenes, and
then hurrying back with Elise to their chairs in the

front row, just as Ranald gave the signal to burn the red lights.

There was the usual confusion in the dressing-room, the tea-house having been taken for that purpose. There was more than usual in some instances, for while the fête had been planned for some time, the tableaux were an afterthought, and many details had been overlooked. Still, with slight delays, they moved along toward a successful finish.

Group by group posed for its particular picture and returned to seats in the audience to enjoy the remainder of the performance. At last only three people were left in the tea-house, and Miss Allison sent Keith, Rob, Phil, and Lieutenant Logan before the curtain, with instructions to sing one of the longest songs they knew and two encores, while Gibbs repaired the prow of the funeral barge. Some one had used it for a step-ladder, and had broken it.

Mary, waiting in the audience till the quartette had finished its first song, did not appear on the scene behind the curtain until Malcolm was dressed in his black robe and long white beard and wig, and Lloyd was laid out on the black bier.

"Stay just as you are," whispered Miss Allison.

" It's perfect. I'm going out into the audience to enjoy the effect as the curtain rises."

As she passed Miss Casey, the elocutionist, she felt some one catch her sleeve. " I've left that copy of Tennyson at the house," she gasped. " What shall I do ? "

" I'll run and get it," volunteered Elise in a whisper, and promptly started off. Mary, standing back in the shadow of a tall lilac bush, clasped her hands in silent admiration of the picture. It was wonderful how the moonlight transformed everything. Here was the living, breathing poem itself before her. She forgot it was Lloyd and Malcolm posing in makeshift costumes on a calico-covered dry goods box. It seemed the barge itself, draped all in blackest samite, going upward with the flood, that day that there was dole in Astolat. While she gazed like one in a dream, Lloyd half-opened her eyes, to peep at the old boatman.

" I wish they'd hurry," she said, in a low tone. " I never felt so foolish in my whole life."

" And never looked more beautiful," Malcolm answered, trying to get another glimpse of her without changing his pose.

" Sh," she whispered back, saucily. " You forget that you are dumb. You mustn't say a word."

"I will," he answered, in a loud whisper. "For even if I were really dumb I think I should find my voice to tell you that with your hair rippling down on that cloth of gold in the moonlight, and all in white, with that lily in your hand, you look like an angel, and I'm in the seventh heaven to be here with you in this boat."

"And with you in that white hair and beard I feel as if it were Fathah Time paying me compliments," said Lloyd, her cheeks dimpling with amusement. "Hush! It's time for me to look dead," she warned, as the applause followed the last encore. "Don't say anything to make me laugh. I'm trying to look as if I had died of a broken heart."

Elise darted back just as the prompter's bell rang, and Mary, turning to follow her to their seats in the audience, saw Miss Casey tragically throw up her hands, with a horrified exclamation. It was not the copy of Tennyson Elise had brought her. In her haste she had snatched up a volume of essays bound in the same blue and gold.

"Go on!" whispered Malcolm, sternly. "Say something. At least go out and explain the tableau in your own words. There are lots of people who won't know what we are aiming at."

Miss Casey only wrung her hands. " Oh, I can't! I can't!" she answered, hoarsely. " I couldn't think of a word before all those people!" As the curtain drew slowly apart, she covered her face with her hands and sank back out of sight in the shrubbery.

The curtain-shifter had answered the signal of the prompter's bell, which at Miss Allison's direction was to be rung immediately after the last applause. Neither knew of the dilemma.

A long-drawn " O-o-oh " greeted the beautiful tableau, and then there was a silence that made Miss Allison rise half-way in her seat, to see what had become of the interpreter. Then she sank back again, for a clear, strong voice, not Miss Casey's, took up the story.

> " And that day there was dole in Astolat.
> Then rose the dumb old servitor, and the dead,
> Oared by the dumb, went upward with the flood."

She did not know who had sprung to the rescue, but Joyce, who recognized Mary's voice, felt a thrill of pride that she was doing it so well. It was better than Miss Casey's rendering, for it was without any professional frills and affectations; just the simple story told in the simplest way by one who

"A LONG-DRAWN 'O-O-OH' GREETED THE BEAUTIFUL TABLEAU"

felt to the fullest the beauty of the picture and the music of the poem.

The red lights flared up, and again the exclamation of pleasure swept through the audience, for Lloyd, lying on the black bier with her hair rippling down and the lily in her hand, might indeed have been the dead Elaine, so ethereal and fair she seemed in that soft glow. Three times the curtains were parted, and even then the enthusiastic guests kept applauding.

There was a rush from the seats, and half a dozen admiring friends pushed between the curtains to offer congratulations. But before they reached her, Lloyd had rolled off her bier to catch Mary in an impulsive hug, crying, " You were a perfect darling to save the day that way! Wasn't she, Malcolm? It was wondahful that you happened to know it! "

The next moment she had turned to Judge Moore and Alex Shelby and the ladies who were with them, to explain how Mary had had the presence of mind and the ability to throw herself into Miss Casey's place on the spur of the moment, and turn a failure into a brilliant success. The congratulations and compliments which she heard on every side were very sweet to Mary's ears, and when Phil came up a little later to tell her that she was a brick and the heroine of the evening, she laughed happily.

" Where is the fair Elaine? " he asked next. " I see her boat is empty. Can you tell me where she has drifted? "

" No," answered Mary, so eager to be of service that she was ready to tell all she knew. " She was here with Sir Feal till just a moment ago."

" Sir Feal! " echoed Phil, in amazement.

" Oh, I forgot that you don't know the Princess play. I meant Mister Malcolm. While so many people were in here congratulating us and shaking hands, I heard him say something to her in an undertone, and then he sang sort of under his breath, you know, so that nobody else but me heard him, that verse from the play:

> " ' Go bid the Princess in the tower
> Forget all thought of sorrow.
> Her true love will return to her
> With joy on some glad morrow.'

" Then he bent over her and said still lower, ' By *my* calendar it's the glad morrow *now,* Princess.'

" He went on just like he was in the play, you know. I suppose they have rehearsed it so much that it is sort of second nature for them to talk in that old-time way, like kings and queens used to do."

"Maybe," answered Phil. "Then what did *she* say?" he demanded, frowning.

"I don't know. She walked off toward the house with him, and that's the last I saw of them. Why, what's the matter?"

"Oh, nothing!" he replied, with a shrug of his shoulders. "Nothing's the matter, little Vicar. *Let us keep inflexible, and fortune will at last change in our favor.*"

"Now whatever did he mean by that!" exclaimed Mary, as she watched him walk away. It puzzled her all the rest of the evening that he should have met her question with the family motto.

CHAPTER IX.

" SOMETHING BLUE "

A RAINY day followed the lawn fête, such a steady pour that little rivers ran down the window-panes, and the porches had to be abandoned. But nobody lamented the fact that they were driven indoors. Rob and Joyce began a game of chess in the library. Lloyd and Phil turned over the music in the cabinet until they found a pile of duets which they both knew, and began to try them, first to the accompaniment of the piano, then the harp.

Mary, sitting in the hall where she could see both the chess-players and the singers, waited in a state of bliss to be summoned to the sewing-room. Only that morning it had been discovered that there was enough pink chiffon left, after the bridesmaids' gowns were completed, to make her a dress, and the seamstress was at work upon it now. So it was a gay, rose-colored world to Mary this morning, despite the leaden skies and pouring rain outside. Not only was she to have a dress, the material for which had actually been brought from Paris, but she was to have little pink satin slippers like the bridesmaids, and she was to have a proud place in the wedding itself. When the bridal party came down the stairs, it was to be her privilege to swing wide the gate of roses for them to pass through.

Joyce had designed the gate. It was to be a double one, swung in the arch between the hall and the drawing-room, and it would take hundreds of roses to make it, the florist said.

In Mary's opinion the office of gate-opener was more to be desired than that of bridesmaid. As she sat listening to the music, curled up in a big hall chair like a contented kitten, she decided that there was nobody in all the world with whom she would change places. There had been times when she would have exchanged gladly with Joyce, thinking of the artist career ahead of her, or with Betty, who was sure to be a famous author some day, or with Lloyd, who seemed to have everything that heart could wish, or with Eugenia with all her lovely presents and trousseau and the new home on the Hudson waiting for her. But just now she was so happy that she wouldn't even have stepped into a fairy-tale.

Presently, through the dripping window-panes, she saw Alec plodding up the avenue under an umbrella, his pockets bulging with mail packages, papers, and letters. Betty, at her window up-stairs, saw him also, and came running down the steps, followed by Eugenia. The old Colonel, hearing the call, " The mail's here," opened the door of his den, and joined the group in the hall where Betty proceeded to sort out the letters. A registered package from Stuart was the first thing that Eugenia tore open, and the others looked up from their letters at her pleased exclamation :

" Oh, it's the charms for the bride's cake! "

" Ornaments for the top? " asked Rob, as she lifted the layer of jeweller's cotton and disclosed a small gold thimble, and a narrow wedding-ring.

" No! Who ever heard of such a thing! " she laughed. " Haven't you heard of the traditional charms that must be baked in a bride's cake? It is a token of the fate one may expect who finds it in his slice of cake. Eliot taught me the old rhyme :

" 'Four tokens must the bridescake hold :
A silver shilling and a ring of gold,
A crystal charm good luck to symbol,
And for the spinster's hand a thimble.'

" Eliot firmly believes that the tokens are a prophecy, for years ago, at her cousin's wedding in England, she got the spinster's thimble. The girl who found the ring was married within the year, and the one who found the shilling shortly came into an inheritance. True, it didn't amount to much, — about five pounds, — but the coincidence firmly convinced Eliot of the truth of the superstition. In this country people usually take a dime instead of a shilling, but I told Stuart that I wanted to follow the custom strictly to the letter. And look what a dear he is! Here is a *bona fide* English shilling, that he took the trouble to get for me."

Phil took up the bit of silver she had placed beside the thimble and the ring, and looked it over critically. " Well, I'll declare! " he exclaimed. " That was Aunt Patricia's old shilling! I'd swear to it. See the way the hole is punched, just between those two ugly old heads? And I remember the dent just below the date. Looks as if some one had tried to bite it. Aunt Patricia used to keep it in her treasure-box with her gold beads and other keepsakes."

The old Colonel, who had once had a fad for collecting coins, and owned a large assortment, held out his hand for it. Adjusting his glasses, he examined it carefully. "Ah! Most interesting," he observed. "Coined in the reign of ' Bloody Mary,' and bearing the heads of Queen Mary and King Philip. You remember this shilling is mentioned in Butler's ' Hudibras: '

> "' Still amorous and fond and billing,
> Like Philip and Mary on a shilling.'

"You couldn't have a more appropriate token for your cake, my dear," he said to Eugenia with a smile. Then he laid it on the table, and taking up his papers, passed back into his den.

"That's the first time I ever heard my name in a poem," said Phil. "By rights I ought to draw that shilling in my share of cake. If I do I shall take it as a sign that history is going to repeat itself, and shall look around for a ladye-love named Mary. Now I know a dozen songs with that name, and such things always come in handy when ' a frog he would a-wooing go.' There's ' My Highland Mary ' and ' Mary of Argyle,' and

'Mistress Mary, quite contrary,' and 'Mary, call the cattle home, across the sands of Dee!'"

As he rattled thoughtlessly on, nothing was farther from his thoughts than the self-conscious little Mary just behind him. Nobody saw her face grow red, however, for Lloyd's exclamation over the last token made every one crowd around her to see.

It was a small heart-shaped charm of crystal, probably intended for a watch-fob. There was a four-leaf clover, somehow mysteriously imbedded in the centre.

"That ought to be doubly lucky," said Eugenia. "Oh, *what* a dear Stuart was to take so much trouble to get the very nicest things. They couldn't be more suitable."

"Eugenia," asked Betty, "have you thought of that other rhyme that brides always consider? You know you should wear

> "'Something old, something new,
> Something borrowed, something blue.'"

"Yes, Eliot insisted on that, too. The whole outfit will, itself, be something new, the lace that was on my mother's wedding-gown will be the something old. I thought I'd borrow a hairpin apiece from you girls, and I haven't decided **yet** about the something blue."

" No," objected Lloyd. " The borrowed articles ought to be something really valuable. Let **me** lend you my little pearl clasps to fasten your veil, and then for the something blue, there is your turquoise butterfly. You can slip it on somewhere, undah the folds of lace."

" What a lot of fol-de-rol there is about a wedding," said Rob. " As if it made a particle of difference whether you wear pink or green! *Why* must it be blue? "

There was an indignant protest from all the girls, and Rob made his escape to the library, calling to Joyce to come and finish the game of chess.

That evening, Mary, sitting on the floor of the library in front of the Poets' Corner, took down volume after volume to scan its index. She was looking for the songs Phil had mentioned, which contained her name. At the same time she also kept watch for the name of Philip. She remembered she had read some lines one time about " Philip my King."

As she pored over the poems in the dim light, for only the shaded lamp on the central table was burning, she heard steps on the porch outside. **The** rain had stopped early in the afternoon, and the porches had dried so that the hammocks and chairs could be put out again. Now voices sounded just outside the window where she sat, and the creaking of a screw in the post told that some one was sitting in the hammock. Evidently it was Lloyd, for Phil's voice sounded nearer the window. He had seated himself in the armchair that always stood in that niche, and was tuning a guitar. As soon as it was keyed up to his satisfaction, he began thrumming on it, a sort of running accompaniment to their conversation.

It did not occur to Mary that she was eavesdropping, for they were talking of impersonal things, just the trifles of the hour; and she caught only a word now and then as she scanned the story of Enoch Arden. The name Philip, in it, had arrested her attention.

" I think the maid of honor ought to wear something blue as well as the bride," remarked Phil.

" Why? " asked Lloyd.

There was such a long pause that Mary looked up, wondering why he did not answer.

" *Why?* " asked Lloyd again.

Phil thrummed on a moment longer, and then began playing in a soft minor key, and his answer, when it finally came, seemed at first to have no connection with what he had been talking about.

" Do you remember when we were in Arizona, the picnic we had at Hole-in-the-rock, and the story that that old Norwegian told about Alaka, the gambling god, who lost his string of precious turquoises and even his eyes? "

" Yes."

Mary looked up from her book, listening alertly. The mystery of years was about to be explained.

" Well, do you remember a conversation you had with Joyce about it afterward, in which you called the turquoise the ' friendship stone,' because it was true blue? And you said it was a pity that some people you knew, not a thousand miles away, couldn't go to the School of the Bees, and learn that line from Watts about Satan finding mischief for idle hands to do. And Joyce said yes, it was too bad for a fine fellow to get into trouble just because he was a drone, and had no ambition to make anything of himself; that if Alaka had gone to the School of the Bees he wouldn't have lost his eyes. And then you said that if somebody kept on he would at least lose his turquoises. Do you remember all that? "

The screw in the post stopped creaking as Lloyd

sat straight up in the hammock to exclaim in astonishment: "Yes, I remembah, but how undah the sun, Phil Tremont, do *you* happen to know anything about that convahsation? You were not there."

"No, but little Mary Ware was. She didn't have the faintest idea that you meant me, and that Sunday morning when I called at the Wigwam for the last time to make my apologies and farewells, and you were not there, she told me all about it like the blessed little chatterbox that she was. Then, when I saw plainly that I had forfeited my right to your friendship, I did not wait to say good-by, just left a message for you with Mary. I knew she would attempt to deliver it, but I have wondered many times since if she gave it in the words I told her. Of course I couldn't expect you to remember the exact words after all this time."

"But it happens that I do," answered Lloyd. "She said, 'Alaka has lost his precious turquoises, but he will win them back again some day.'"

"Did you understand what I meant, Lloyd?"

"Well, I — I guessed at yoah meaning."

"Mary unwittingly did me a good turn that morning. She was an angel unawares, for she showed me myself as you saw me, a drone in the hive, with no ambition, and the gambling fever in my veins making a fool of me. I went away vowing I would win back your respect and make myself worthy of your friendship, and I can say honestly that I have kept that vow. Soon after, while I was out on that first surveying trip I came across some unset stones for a mere song. This little turquoise was among them." He took the tiny stone from his pocket and held it out on his palm, so that the light streaming out from the library fell across it.

"I have carried it ever since. Many a time it has reminded me of you and your good opinion I was trying to win back. I've had lots of temptations to buck against, and there have been times when they almost downed me, but I say it in all humility, Lloyd, this little bit of turquoise kept me 'true blue,' and I've lived straight enough to ask you to take it now, in token that you do think me worthy of your friendship. When I heard Eugenia talking about wearing something blue at the wedding, I had a fancy that it would be an appropriate thing for the maid of honor to do, too."

Lloyd took the little stone he offered, and held it up to the light.

"It certainly is true blue," she said, with a smile,

"and I'm suah you are too, now. I didn't need this to tell me how well you've been doing since you left Arizona. We've heard a great deal about yoah successes from Cousin Carl."

"Then let me have it set in a ring for you," he added. "There will be plenty of time before the wedding."

"No," she answered, hastily. "I couldn't do that. Papa Jack wouldn't like it. He wouldn't allow me to accept anything from a man in the way of jewelry, you know. I couldn't take it as a ring. Now just this little unset stone" — she hesitated. "Just this bit of a turquoise that you say cost only a trifle, I'm suah he wouldn't mind that. I'll tell him it's just my friendship stone."

"What a particular little maid of honor you are!" he exclaimed. "How many girls of seventeen do you know who would take the trouble to go to their fathers with a trifle like that, and make a careful explanation about it? Besides, you can't tell him that it is *only* a friendship stone. I want it to mean more than that to you, Lloyd. I want it to stand for a great deal more between us. Don't you see how I care — how I must have cared all this time, to let the thought of you make such a difference in my life?"

There was no mistaking the deep tenderness of his voice or the earnestness of his question. Lloyd felt the blood surge up in her face and her heart throbbed so fast she could hear it beat. But she hastily thrust back the proffered turquoise, saying, in confusion:

"Then I can't wear it! Take it back, please; I promised Papa Jack —"

"Promised him what?" asked Phil, as she hesitated.

"Well, it's rathah hard to explain," she began in much confusion, "unless you knew the story of 'The Three Weavahs.' Then you'd undahstand."

"But I don't know it, and I'd rather like an explanation of some kind. I think you'll have to make it clear to me why you can't accept it, and what it was you promised your father."

"Oh, I can't tell it to make it sound like anything," she began, desperately. "It was like this. No, I can't tell it. Come in the house, and I'll get the book and let you read it for yoahself."

"No, I'd rather hear the reason from your own lips. Besides, some one would interrupt us in there, and I want to understand where I'm 'at' before that happens."

"Well," she began again, "it is a story Mrs.

Walton told us once when our Shadow Club was
in disgrace, because one of the girls eloped, and
we were all in such trouble about it that we vowed
we'd be old maids. Afterward it was the cause
of our forming another club that we called the
'Ordah of Hildegarde.' I'll give you a sawt of
an outline now, if you'll promise to read the entiah
thing aftahward."

"I'll promise," agreed Phil.

"Then, this is it. Once there were three maidens,
of whom it was written in the stahs that each was
to wed a prince, provided she could weave a mantle
that should fit his royal shouldahs as the falcon's
feathahs fit the falcon. Each had a mirror beside
her loom like the Lady of Shalott's in which the
shadows of the world appeahed.

"One maiden wove in secret, and falling in love
with a page who daily passed her mirror, imagined
him to be a prince, and wove her web to fit his unworthy shouldahs. Of co'se when the real prince
came it was too small, and so she missed the happiness that was written for her in the stahs.

"The second squandahed her warp of gold first
on one, then anothah, weaving mantles for any
one who happened to take her fancy — a shepherd
boy and a troubador, a student and a knight.

When her prince rode by she had nothing left to offah him, so she missed *her* life's happiness.

"But the third had a deah old fathah like Papa Jack, and he gave her a silvah yahdstick on which was marked the inches and ells that a true prince ought to be. And he warned her like this:

"'Many youths will come to thee, each begging, "Give *me* the royal mantle, Hildegarde. *I* am the prince the stahs have destined for thee." And with honeyed words he'll show thee how the mantle in the loom is just the length to fit his shouldahs. But let him not persuade thee to cut it loose and give it to him as thy young fingahs will be fain to do. Weave on anothah yeah and yet anothah, till thou, a woman grown, can measuah out a perfect web, moah ample than these stripling youths could carry, but which will fit thy prince in faultlessness, as the falcon's feathahs fit the falcon.'

"Then Hildegarde took the silvah yahdstick and said, 'You may trust me, fathah. I will not cut the golden warp from out the loom, until I, a woman grown, have woven such a web as thou thyself shalt say is worthy of a prince's wearing.' (That's what I promised Papa Jack.)

"Of co'se it turned out, that one day with her

fathah's blessing light upon her, she rode away beside the prince, and evah aftah all her life was crowned with happiness, as it had been written for her in the stahs."

There was a long pause when she finished, so long that the silence began to grow painful. Then Phil said, slowly:

"I understand now. Would you mind telling me what the measure was your father gave you that your prince must be?"

"There were three notches. He must be clean and honahable and strong."

There was another long pause before Phil said, "Well, I wouldn't be measuring up to that second notch if I asked you to break your promise to your father, and you wouldn't do it even if I did. So there's nothing more for me to say at present. But I'll ask this much. You'll keep the turquoise if we count it merely a friendship stone, won't you?"

"Yes, I'll be glad to do that. And I'll weah it at the wedding if you want me to. as my bit of something blue. I'll slip it down into my glove."

"Thank you," he answered, then added, after a pause: "And I suppose there's another thing.

That yardstick keeps all the other fellows at a distance, too. That's something to be cheerful over. But you mark my words — I'm doing a bit of prophesying now — when your real prince comes you'll know him by this: he'll come singing this song. Listen."

Picking up his guitar again, he struck one full deep chord and began singing softly the " Bedouin Love-song," " From the desert I come to thee." The refrain floated tremulously through the library window.

> " Till the stars are old,
> And the sun grows cold,
> And the leaves of the judgment
> Book unfold."

It brought back the whole moonlighted desert to Lloyd, with the odor of orange-blossoms wafted across it, as it had been on two eventful occasions they rode over it together. She sat quite still in the hammock, with the bit of turquoise clasped tight in her hand. It was hard to listen to such a beautiful voice unmoved. It thrilled her as no song had ever done before.

As it floated into the library, it thrilled Mary also, but in a different way; for with a guilty

start she realized that she had been listening to
something not meant for her to hear.

"Oh, what have I done! What have I done!"
she whispered to herself, dropping the book and
noiselessly wringing her hands. She could hear
voices on the stairs now. Eugenia and Betty were
coming down, and Rob's whistle down the avenue
told that he was on his way to join them. Too
ashamed to face any one just then, and afraid that
her guilty face would betray the fact to Phil and
Lloyd that she shared their secret, she hurried out
of the library and up to her room, where Joyce
was rearranging her hair. In response to Joyce's
question about her coming up so early in the evening, she said she had thought of something she
wanted to write in her journal. But when Joyce
had gone down she did not begin writing immediately. Turning down the lamp until the room
was almost in darkness, she sat with her elbows
on the window-sill staring out into the night.

"I never *meant* to do it!" she kept explaining
to her conscience. "It just did itself. It seemed
all right to listen at first, when they were talking
about things I had a right to know, and then I
got so interested, it was like reading a story, and
I couldn't go away because I forgot there was such

a person living as *me*. But Lloyd mightn't understand how it was. She'd scorn to be an eaves-
dropper herself, and she'd scorn and despise me
if she knew that I just sat there like a graven
image and listened to Phil the same as propose
to her."

Hitherto Mary had looked upon Malcolm as
Lloyd's especial knight, and had planned to be
his valiant champion should need for her services
ever arise. But this put matters in a different
light. All her sympathies were enlisted in Phil's
behalf now. She liked Phil the best, and she wanted
him to have whatever he wanted. He had called her
his "angel unawares," and she wished she could
do something to further deserve that title. Then
she began supposing things.

Suppose she should come tripping down the
stairs some day (this would be sometime in the
future, of course, when Lloyd's promise to her
father was no longer binding) and should find Phil
pacing the room with impatient strides because
the maid of honor had gone off with Sir Feal to
the opera or somewhere, in preference to him, on
account of some misunderstanding. "The little
rift within the lute" would be making the best

man's music mute, and now would be her time to
play angel unawares again.

She would trip in lightly, humming a song per-
haps, and finding him moody and downcast, would
begin the conversation with some appropriate quotation. In looking through the dictionary the day
before, her eye had caught one from Shakespeare,
which she had stored away in her memory to use
on some future occasion. Yes, that one would be
very appropriate to begin the conversation. She
would go up to him and say, archly :

> " My lord leans wondrously to discontent.
> His comfortable temper has forsook him."

With that a smile would flit across his stern
features, and presently he would be moved to confide in her, and she would encourage him. Then,
she didn't know yet exactly in what way it could
come about, she would do something to bring the
two together again, and wipe out the bitter misunderstanding.

It was a very pleasing dream. That and others
like it kept her sitting by the window till nearly
bedtime. Then, just before the girls came up-
stairs, she turned up the lamp and made an entry
in her journal. With the fear that some prying

eye might some day see that page, she omitted all names, using only initials. It would have puzzled the Sphinx herself to have deciphered that entry, unless she had guessed that the initials stood for titles instead of names. The last paragraph concluded: "It now lies between Sir F. and the B. M., but I think it will be the B. M. who will get the mantle, for Sir F. and his brother have gone away on a yachting trip. The M. of H. does not know that I know, and the secret weighs heavy on my mind."

She was in bed when the girls came up, but the door into the next room stood open and she heard Betty say, "Oh, we forgot to give you Alex Shelby's message, Lloyd. Joyce and I met him on our way to the post-office. He was walking with Bernice. He sent his greetings to the fair Elaine. He fairly raved over the way you looked in that moonlight tableau."

"It was evident that Bernice didn't enjoy his raptures very much," added Joyce. "Her face showed that she was not only bored, but displeased."

"I can imagine it," said Lloyd. "Really, girls, I think this is a serious case with Bernice. She seems to think moah of Mistah Shelby than any one who has evah gone to see her, and she is old enough now to have it mean something. She's neahly twenty, you know. I do hope he thinks as much of her as she does of him."

"There!" whispered Mary to herself, nodding wisely in the darkness of her room, as if to an unseen listener. "I knew it! I told you so! All the king's horses and all the king's men couldn't make me believe she'd stoop to such a thing as that nasty Bernice Howe insinuated. She's a maid of honor in every way!"

CHAPTER X.

" A COON HUNT "

THE morning after the arrival of the rest of the bridal party, Betty was out of bed at the first sound of any one stirring in the servants' quarters. She and Lloyd had given up their rooms to the new guests, and moved back into the sewing-room together. Now in order not to awaken Lloyd she tiptoed out to the little vine-covered balcony, through the window that opened into it from the sewing-room. She was in her nightgown, for she could not wait to dress, when she was so eager to find out what kind of a day Eugenia was to have for her wedding.

Not a cloud was in sight. It was as perfect as only a June morning can be, in Kentucky. The fresh smell of dewy roses and new-mown grass mingled with the pungent smoke of the wood fire, just beginning to curl up in blue rings from the kitchen chimney. Soft twitterings and jubilant bird-calls followed the flash of wings from tree to tree. She peeped out between the thick mass of wistaria vines, across the grassy court, formed by the two rear wings of the house, to another balcony opposite the one in which she stood. It opened off Eugenia's room, and was almost hidden by a climbing rose, which made a perfect bride's bower, with its gorgeous full-blown Gloire Dijon roses.

Stray rhymes and words suggestive of music and color and the morning's glory began to flit through her mind as she stood there, as if a little poem were about to start to life with a happy fluttering of wings; a madrigal of June. But in a few moments she slipped back into the house through the window, put on her kimono and slippers, and gathering up her journal in one hand and pen and ink with the other, she stole back to the balcony again. The seamstress had left her sewing-chair out there the afternoon she finished Mary's dress, and it still stood there, with the lap-board beside it. Taking the board on her knees, and opening her journal upon it, Betty perched her ink-bottle on the balcony railing and began to write. She knew there would be no time later in the day for her to bring her record up-to-date, and she did not want to let the happenings pile up unrecorded. She was afraid she might leave out something she wanted to include, and she had found that the trivial conversations and the trifles she noted were often the things which recalled a scene most vividly, and almost made it seem to live again. She began her narrative just where she had left off, so that it made a continuous story.

"We didn't settle down to anything yesterday morning. Phil went to town with Papa Jack directly after breakfast, and we girls just strolled up and down the avenue and talked. It was delightfully cool under the locusts, and we knew it would be our last morning with Eugenia; that after the arrival of the rest of the bridal party, everything would be in confusion until after the wedding, and then she would never be Eugenia Forbes again. She would be Mrs. Stuart Tremont.

"She told us that her being married wouldn't make any difference, that she'd always be the same to us. But it's bound to make a difference. A married woman can't be interested in the same things that young girls are. Her husband is bound to come first in her consideration.

"Joyce asked her if it didn't make her feel queer to know that her wedding-day was coming closer and closer, and quoted that line from 'The Siege of Lucknow,' — '*Day by day the Bengal tiger nearer*

drew and closer crept.' She said she'd have a fit if
she knew her wedding-day was creeping up on her
that way. Eugenia was horrified to have her talk
that way, and said that it was because she didn't
know Stuart, and didn't know what it meant to
care enough for a man to be glad to join her life
to his, forever and ever. There was such a light in
her eyes as she talked about him, that we didn't say
anything more for awhile, just wondered how it
must feel to be so supremely happy as she is. There
is no doubt about it, he is certainly the one written
for her in the stars, for he measures up to every
ideal of hers, as faultlessly ' as the falcon's feathers
fit the falcon.'

" We had heard so much from her and Phil about
Doctor Miles Bradford, Stuart's friend who is
coming with him to be one of the ushers, that we
dreaded meeting him. When she told us that he is
from Boston and belongs to one of its most ex-
clusive families, and is very conventional, and
twenty-five years old, Joyce nicknamed him ' The
Pilgrim Father,' and vowed she woudn't have him
for her attendant; that I had to take him and let her
walk in with Rob. She said she'd shock him with
her wild west slang and uncivilized ways, and that

I was the literary lady of the establishment, and would know how to entertain such a personage.

"I was just as much afraid of him as she was, and wanted Rob myself, so we squabbled over it all the way up and down the avenue. We were walking five abreast, swinging hands. When we got to the gate we saw some one coming up the road, and we all stood in a row, peeping out between the bars till we saw that it was Rob himself. Then Joyce said that we would make him decide the matter — that we'd all put our hands through the bars as if we had something in them, and make him choose which he'd take, right or left. If he said right, I could have him for my attendant and she'd take Doctor Bradford, but if he said left I'd have to put up with the Pilgrim Father, and she'd take Rob.

"He came along bareheaded, swinging his hat in his hand, and we were so busy explaining to him that he was to choose which hand he'd take, right or left, that we did not notice that he had a kodak hidden behind his hat. He held it up in front of him, and bowed and scraped and did all sorts of ridiculous things to keep us from noticing what he was doing, till all of a sudden we heard the shutter click and he gave a whoop and said, 'There! That will be one of the best pictures in my collection.

"'ALL YOU GIRLS STANDING WITH YOUR HANDS STUCK
THROUGH THE BARS'"

All you girls standing with your hands stuck through the bars, like monkeys at the Zoo, begging for peanuts. I don't know whether to call it " Behind the Bars," or " Don't Feed the Animals." '

" Then Lloyd said he shouldn't come in for making such a speech, and he sat down on the grass and began to sing in a ridiculous way, the old song that goes :

> " ' Oh, angel, sweet angel, I pray thee
> Set the beautiful gates ajar.'

" He was off the key, as he usually is when he sings without an accompaniment, and it was so funny, such a howl of a song, that we laughed till the tears came. Then he said he'd name the picture ' At the Gate of Paradise,' and make a foot-note to the effect that she was a Peri, if she'd let him in.

" After awhile she said she'd let him in to Paradise if he could name one good deed he'd ever done that had benefited human kind. He said certainly he could, and that he wouldn't have to dig it up from the dead past. He could give it to her hot from the griddle, for only ten minutes before he had completed arrangements for the evening's entertainment of the bridal party.

" Lloyd opened the gate in a hurry then, and fairly begged him to come in, for we had been wild all week to know what godmother had decided upon. She only laughed when we teased her to tell us, and said we'd see. We were sure it would be something very elegant and formal. Maybe a real grown-up affair, with an orchestra from town and distinguished strangers to meet the three fathers, Eugenia's, Stuart's and the Pilgrim F.

" We couldn't believe Rob when he told us that we were to go on a *coon hunt,* and went racing up to the house to ask godmother herself.

" And she said yes, she was sure they would enjoy a glimpse of real country Southern life, and some of our informal fun, far more than the functions they could attend any time in the East. Besides she wanted everybody to keep in mind that we were still little schoolgirls, even if we were to be bridesmaids, and that was why she was taking us all off to the woods for an old-time country frolic, instead of having a grand dinner or a formal dance.

" Then Rob asked us if we didn't want to beg his pardon for doubting his word, but Lloyd told him no, that

> " ' The truth itself is not believed
> From one who often has deceived.'

" Then we tried to make him choose which he'd have, right or left, and held out our hands again, but he said he knew that some great question of choice was being involved, and that he would not assume the responsibility. That we'd have to draw straws, if we wanted to decide anything. So Eugenia held two blades of grass between her palms, and Joyce drew the longest one. I couldn't help groaning, for that meant that the Pilgrim Father must fall to my lot.

"But it didn't seem so bad after I met him. They all came out on the three o'clock train with Phil. When the carriage came up from the station we had a grand jubilee. Cousin Carl seemed so glad to get back to the Valley, but no gladder than everybody was to see him. Stuart is so much like Phil that we felt as if we were already acquainted with him. He is very boyish-looking and young, but there is something so dignified and gentle in his manner that one feels he is cut out to be a staid old family physician, and that in time he will grow into the love and confidence of his patients like Maclaren's Doctor of the Old School. But dear old Doctor Tremont is the flower of *that* family. We all fell in love with him the moment we saw him. It is easy to see what he has been to his boys. The very tone in which they call him ' Daddy ' shows how they adore him; and he is so sweet and tender with Eugenia.

"Contrasted with him and Cousin Carl, I must say that the Pilgrim Father is not a suitable name for Doctor Bradford. Really, with his smooth shaven face, and clear ruddy complexion like an Englishman's, he doesn't seem much older than Malcolm. Still his dignity is rather awe-full, and his grave manner and Boston accent make him seem sort of foreign, so different from the boys whom we have always known. We were afraid at first that godmother had made a great mistake in planning to take him on a coon hunt. But it turned out that she was right, as she always is. He told us afterward he had never enjoyed anything so much in all his life.

"It was just eight o'clock when we set out on the hunt last night. A big hay-wagon drove up to the door with the party from The Beeches already stowed away in it, sitting flat on the hay in the bottom. Mrs. Walton was with them, and Miss Allison and Katie Mallard and her father, and several others they had picked up on the way.

"While they were laughing and talking and everybody was being introduced Alec came driving up from the barn with another big wagon, and we all piled into it except Lloyd and Rob, Joyce and Phil. They were on horseback and kept alongside of us as outriders. The moon hadn't come up, but the starlight was so bright that the road gleamed like a white ribbon ahead of us, and we sang most of the way to the woods.

" Old Unc' Jefferson led the procession on his white mule, with three lanky coon dogs following. They struck the trail before we reached our stopping-place, and went dashing off into the woods. Unc' Jefferson fairly rolled off his old mule, and threw the rope bridle over the first fence-post, and went crashing through the underbrush after them. The wagons kept on a few rods farther and landed us on the creek bank, up by the black bridge.

" It seemed as if the whole itinerary of the hunt had been planned for our especial benefit, for just as we reached the creek the moon began to roll up through the trees like a great golden mill-wheel, and we could see our way about in the woods. Evidently the coon's home was in some hollow near our stopping-place, for instead of staying in the dense beech woods, up where it would have been hard for us to climb, the first dash of the dogs sent him scurrying toward the row of big sycamores that overhang the creek.

" It whizzed by us so fast that at first we did not know what had passed us till the dogs came tumbling after at breakneck speed. They were such old hands at the game that they gave their quarry a bad time of it for awhile, turning and doubling on his tracks till we were almost as excited and bewildered as the poor coon. Little Mary Ware just stood and wrung her hands, and once when the dogs were almost on him she teetered up and down on her tiptoes and squealed.

" All of a sudden the coon dodged to one side and disappeared. We thought he had escaped, but a little later on we heard the dogs baying frantically farther down the creek, and Rob shouted that they had treed him, and for everybody to hurry up if they wanted to be in at the death. So away we went, helter-skelter, in a wild race down the creek bank, godmother, Papa Jack, Cousin Carl, and everybody. It was a rough scramble, and as we pitched over rolling stones, and caught at bushes to pull ourselves up, and swung down holding on to the saplings, I wondered what Doctor Bradford would think of our tomboy ways.

" Nobody waited to be helped. It was every fellow for himself, we were in such a hurry to get to the coon. Lloyd kept far in the lead, ahead of

everybody, and Joyce walked straight up a steep
bank as if she had been a fly. When we got to the
tree where the dogs were howling and baying we
had to look a long time before we could see the
coon. Then all we could distinguish was the shine
of its eyeballs, for it crouched so flat against the
limb that it seemed a part of the bark. It was away
out on the tip-end of one of the highest branches.

" The only way to get it was to shake it down,
and to our surprise, before we knew who had volunteered, we saw Doctor Bradford, in his immaculate
white flannels, throw off his coat and go shinning
up the tree like an acrobat in a circus. He had to
shake and shake the limb before he could dislodge
the coon, but at last it let go, and the dogs had it
before it fairly touched the ground. We girls didn't
wait to see what they did with it, but stuck our
fingers in our ears and tore back to the wagons.
Rob made fun of Lloyd when she said she didn't
see why they couldn't have coon hunts without coon
killings, and that they ought to have made the dogs
let go. They had had the fun of catching it, and
they ought to be satisfied with that.

" Joyce whispered to me that the hunt had had
one desirable result. It had limbered up the Pilgrim
Father so thoroughly, that he couldn't be stiff and

dignified again after his acrobatic feat. It really did make a difference, for after that he was one of the jolliest men in the party.

"As it was out of season and old Unc' Jefferson didn't care for the coons, he called off the dogs after they had caught one, to show us what the sport was like, and then he built us a grand camp-fire on the creek bank, and we had what Mrs. Walton called the sequel. She and Miss Allison and godmother made coffee and unpacked the hampers we had brought with us. There was beaten biscuit and fried chicken and iced watermelon, and all sorts of good things. As we ate, the moon came up higher and higher, and silvered the white trunks of the sycamores till they looked like a row of ghosts standing with outstretched arms along the creek. It was so lovely there above the water. All the sweet woodsy smells of fern and mint and fallen leaves seem stronger after nightfall. Everybody enjoyed the feast so much, and was in such high spirits that we all felt a shade of regret that it had to come to an end so soon.

"There were two boats down by the bridge which we found that Rob had had sent over that morning for the occasion. They had brought the oars over in the wagon. Pretty soon we saw Eugenia and

"'THEY STEPPED IN AND ROWED OFF DOWN THE SHINING
WATERWAY'"

Stuart going down toward one of them, a little white canvas one, and they stepped in and rowed off down the shining waterway. It was only a narrow creek, but the moonlight seemed to glorify it, and we knew that it made them think of that boatride that had been the beginning of their happiness, in far-away Venice.

" The other boat was larger. Allison and Miss Bonham, Phil and Lieutenant Stanley went out in that. The music of their singing, as it floated back to us, was so beautiful, that those of us on the bank stopped talking to listen. When they came back presently, Kitty and Joyce, Rob and Lieutenant Logan pushed out in it for awhile. They sang too.

" When the little boat came back, Doctor Bradford asked Lloyd to go out with him, and she said she would as soon as she had given her chatelaine watch to her father to keep for her. The clasp kept coming unfastened and she was afraid she would lose it."

Here Betty laid down her pen a moment and sat peering dreamily out between the vines. She was about to record a little conversation she had overheard between Lloyd and her father as they stood a moment in the bushes behind her, but paused as she reflected that it would be like betraying a confidence to make an entry of it in her journal. It would be even worse, since it was no confidence of hers, but a matter lying between Lloyd and her father alone.

She sat tapping the rim of the ink-bottle with her pen as she recalled the conversation. " Yes, it's all right for you to go, Lloyd, but wait a moment. Have you my silver yardstick with you to-night, dear?"

" Why of co'se, Papa Jack. What makes you ask such a question?"

" Well," he answered, " there is so much weaving going on around you lately, and weddings are apt to put all sorts of notions into a girl's head. I just wanted to remind you that only village lads and shepherd boys are in sight, probably not even a knight, and the mantle must be worthy of a prince's wearing, you know."

Then Lloyd pretended to be hurt, and Betty could tell from her voice just how she lifted her head with an air of injured dignity.

" Remembah I gave you my promise, suh, the promise of a Lloyd. Isn't that enough?"

" More than enough, my little Hildegarde." As they stepped out of the bushes together Betty saw him playfully pinch her cheek. Then Lloyd went on down the bank. Here Betty took up her pen again.

"When she stepped into the boat the moonlight on her white dress and shining hair made her look almost as ethereal and fair as she had in the Elaine tableau. The boats could only go as far as the shallows, just a little way below the bridge, so they went back and forth a number of times, making such a pretty picture for those who waited on the bank.

"After Doctor Bradford had brought Lloyd back he asked me to go with him, and oh, it was so beautiful out there on the water. I'll enjoy the memory of it as long as I live. At first I couldn't think of anything to say, and the more I tried to think of something that would interest a man like him, the more embarrassed I grew. It was the first time I had ever tried to talk to any but old men or the home boys.

"After we had rowed a little way in silence he turned to me with the jolliest twinkle in his eyes and asked me why the boat ought to be called the Mayflower. I was *so* surprised, I asked him if that was a riddle, and he said no, but he wondered if I wouldn't feel that it was the Mayflower because I was adrift in it with the Pilgrim Father.

" I was so embarrassed I didn't know what to say, for I couldn't imagine how he had found out that we had called him that. I couldn't have talked to him at all if I had known what Lloyd told me afterward when we had gone to our room. It seems that by some unlucky chance he was left alone with Mary Ware for awhile before dinner. Godmother told her to entertain him, and she proceeded to do so by showing him the collection of all the kodak pictures Rob had taken of us during the house-party. After he left us yesterday morning he went straight to work to develop and print the films he had just taken, and when he brought us the copies that afternoon, we were busy, and he slipped them into the album with the others without saying anything about them. So none of us saw them until Mary came across them in showing them to Doctor Bradford.

" There was the one of us with our hands thrust through the bars, when we were trying to make Rob choose right or left, and one of Joyce and me drawing straws. Neither of us had the slightest idea that he had taken us in that act, and Mary was so surprised that she gave the whole thing away — blurted out what we were doing, before she thought that he was the Pilgrim Father. Then in her con-

fusion, to cover up her mistake, she began to explain as only Mary Ware can, and the more she
explained, the more ridiculous things she told about
us. Doctor Bradford must have found her vastly
entertaining from the way he laughed whenever he
quoted her, which he did frequently.

" I wish she wouldn't be so alarmingly outspoken
when she sings our praises to strangers. She gave
him to understand that I am a full-fledged author
and playwright, the peer of any poet laureate who
ever held a pen; that Lloyd is a combination of
princess and angel and halo-crowned saint, and
Joyce a model big sister and an all-round genius.
How she managed in the short time they were alone
to tell him as much as she did will always remain
a mystery.

" He knew all about Joyce raising bees at the
Wigwam to earn money for her art lessons, and
my nearly going blind at the first house-party, and
why we all wear Tusitala rings. Only time will
reveal what else she told. Maybe, after all, her con-
fidences made things easier, for it gave us something to laugh about right in the beginning, and
that took away the stiff feeling, and we were soon
talking like old friends. By the time the boat
landed I was glad that he had fallen to my lot as

attendant instead of Rob, for he is so much more entertaining. He told about a moonlight ride he had on the Nile last winter when he was in Egypt, and that led us to talking of lotus flowers, and that to Tennyson's poem of the 'Lotus Eaters.' He quoted a verse from it which he said was, to him, one of the best comparisons in English verse.

> " ' There is sweet music here that softer falls
>   Than petals from blown roses on the grass,
>   Or night dews upon still waters, between walls
>   Of shadowy granite in a gleaming pass.
>   *Music that gentlier on the spirit lies*
>   *Than tired eyelids upon tired eyes.*'

" The other boat-load, far down the creek, was singing ' Sweet and low, wind of the western sea,' and he rested on his oars for us to listen. I had often repeated that verse to myself when I closed my eyes after a hard day's study. Nothing falls gentlier than tired eyelids upon tired eyes, and to have him understand the feeling and admire the poem in the same way that I did, was such a pleasant sensation, as if I had come upon a delightful unexplored country, full of pleasant surprises.

" Such thoughts as that about music are the ones I love best, and yet I never would dream of speaking of such things to Rob or Malcolm, who are both old and dear friends.

"After all, the coon hunt proved a very small part of the evening's entertainment, and he must have liked it, for I heard him say to godmother, as he bade her good night, that if this was a taste of real Kentucky life, he would like a steady diet of it all the rest of his days."

CHAPTER XI.

THE FOUR - LEAVED CLOVER

As Betty carefully blotted the last page and placed the stopper in the ink-bottle, the clock in the hall began to strike, and she realized that she must have been writing fully an hour. The whole household was astir now. She would be late to breakfast unless she hurried with her dressing.

Steps on the gravelled path below the balcony made her peep out between the vines. Stuart and Doctor Bradford were coming back from an early stroll about the place. The wistaria clung too closely to the trellis for them to see her, but, as they crossed the grassy court between the two wings, they looked up at Eugenia's balcony opposite. Betty looked too. That bower of golden-hearted roses had drawn her glances more than once that morning. Now in the midst of it, in a morning dress of pink, fresh and fair as a blossom herself, stood Eugenia, reaching up for a half-blown bud above her head. Her sleeves fell back from her graceful white arms, and as she broke the bud from its stem a shower of rose-petals fell on her dusky hair and upturned face.

Then Betty saw that Doctor Bradford had passed on into the house, leaving Stuart standing there with his hat in his hand, smiling up at the beautiful picture above him.

" Good morrow, Juliet," he called, softly. " Happy is the bride the sun shines on. Was there ever such a glorious morning? "

" It's perfect," answered Eugenia, leaning out of her rose bower to smile down at him.

" I wonder if the bride's happiness measures up to the morning," he asked. " Mine does."

For answer she glanced around, her finger on her lips as if to warn him that walls have ears, and then with a light little laugh tossed the rosebud down to him. " Wait! I'll come and tell you," she said.

Betty, gathering up her writing material, saw him catch the rose, touch it to his lips and fasten it in his coat. Then, conscience-smitten that she had seen the little by-play not intended for other eyes, she bolted back into her room through the window, so hurriedly that she struck her head against the sash with a force which made her see stars for several minutes.

The first excitement after breakfast was the arrival of the bride's cake. Aunt Cindy had baked it, the bride herself had stirred the charms into it, but it had been sent to Louisville to be iced. Lloyd called the entire family into the butler's pantry to admire it, as it sat imposingly on a huge silver salver.

" It looks as if it might have come out of the Snow Queen's palace," she said, " instead of the confectionah's. Wouldn't you like to see the place where those snow-rose garlands grow? "

" Somebody take Phil away from it! Quick! " said Stuart. " Once I had a birthday cake iced in pink with garlands of white sugar roses all around it, and he sneaked into the pantry before the party and picked off so many of the roses that it looked as if a mouse had nibbled the edges. Aunt Patricia put him to bed and he missed the party, but we couldn't punish him that way if he should spoil the wedding cake, because we need his services as best man. So we'd better remove him from temptation."

" Look here, son," answered Phil, taking Stuart by the shoulders and pushing him ahead of him.

"When it comes to raking up youthful sins you'd better lie low. 'I could a tale unfold' that would make Eugenia think that this is 'a fatal wedding morn.' If she knew all she wouldn't have you."

"Then you sha'n't tell anything," declared Lloyd. "I'm not going to be cheated out of my share of the wedding, no mattah what a dahk past eithah of you had. Forget it, and come and help us hunt the foah-leaf clovahs that Eugenia wants for the dream-cake boxes."

"What are they?" asked Miles Bradford, as he edged out of the pantry after the others. Mary happened to be the one in front of him, and she turned to answer, pointing to one of the shelves, where lay a pile of tiny heart-shaped boxes, tied with white satin ribbons.

"Each guest is to have one of those," she explained. "There'll be a piece of wedding cake in it, and a four-leaf clover if we can find enough to go around. Most people don't have the clovers, but Eugenia heard about them, and she wants to try all the customs that everybody ever had. You put it under your pillow for three nights, and whatever you dream will come true. If you dream about the same person all three nights, that is the one you will marry."

"Horrible!" exclaimed he, laughing. "Suppose one has nightmares. Will they come true?"

Mary nodded gravely. "Mom Beck says so, and Eliot. So did old Mrs. Bisbee. She's the one that told Eugenia about the clovers. There was one with her piece of cake from her sister's wedding, that she dreamed on nearly fifty years ago. She dreamed of Mr. Bisbee three nights straight ahead, and she said there never was a more fortunate wedding. They'll celebrate their golden anniversary soon."

"Miss Mary," asked her listener, solemnly, "do you girls really believe all these signs and wonders? I have heard more queer superstitions the few hours I have been in this Valley, than in all my life before."

"Oh, no, we don't really believe in them. Only the darkies do that. But you can't help feeling more comfortable when they 'point right' for you than when they don't; like seeing the new moon over your right shoulder, you know. And it's fun to try all the charms. Eugenia says so many brides have done it that it seems a part of the performance, like the veil and the trail and the orange-blossoms."

They passed from the dining-room into the hall, then out on to the front porch, where they stood waiting for Joyce and Eugenia to get their hats. While they waited, Rob Moore joined them, and they explained the quest they were about to start upon.

" Where are you going to take us, Miss Lloyd? " asked Miles Bradford. " According to the old legend the four-leaved clover is to be found only in Paradise."

" Oh, do you know a legend about it? " asked Betty, eagerly. " I've always thought there ought to be one."

" Then you must read the little book, Miss Betty, called ' Abdallah, or the Four-leaved Shamrock.' Abdallah was a son of the desert who spent his life in a search for the lucky shamrock. He had been taught that it was the most beautiful flower of Paradise. One leaf was red like copper, another white like silver, the third yellow like gold, and the fourth was a glittering diamond. When Adam and Eve were driven out of the garden, poor Eve reached out and clutched at a blossom to carry away with her. In her despair she did not notice what she plucked, but, as she passed through the portal, curiosity made her open her hand to look at the flower she had snatched. To her joy it was the shamrock. But while she looked, a gust of wind caught up the diamond leaf and blew it back within the gates, just as they closed behind her. The name of that leaf was Perfect Happiness. That is why men never find it in this world for all their searching. It is to be found only in Paradise."

" Oh, but I don't believe that! " cried Lloyd. " Lots and lots of times I have been perfectly happy, and I am suah that everybody must be at some time or anothah in this world."

" Yes, but you didn't stay happy, did you? " asked Joyce, who had come back in time to hear part of the legend. " We get glimpses of it now and then, as poor Eve did when she opened her hand, but part of it always flies away while we are looking at it. People can be contented all the time, and happy in a mild way, but nobody can be perfectly, radiantly happy all the time, day in and day out. The legend is right. It is only in Paradise that one can find the diamond leaf."

" Joyce talks as if she were a hundred yeahs old," laughed Lloyd, looking up at Doctor Bradford. " Maybe there is some truth in yoah old Oriental legend, but I believe times have changed since Abdallah went a-hunting. Phil and I came across a song the othah day that I want you all to heah. Maybe it will make you change yoah minds."

Phil protested with many grimaces and much nonsense that he "could not sing the old songs now." That he would not "be butchered to make a Roman holiday." But all the time he protested, he was stepping toward the piano in a fantastic exaggerated cake-walk that set his audience to laughing. At the first low notes of the accompaniment, he dropped his foolishness and began to sing in a full, sweet voice that brought the old Colonel to the door of his den to listen. Eliot, packing trunks in the upper hall, leaned over the banister:

"I know a place where the sun is like gold,
  And the cherry blooms burst with snow.
  And down underneath is the loveliest nook
  Where the four-leaf clovers grow.

"One leaf is for hope and one is for faith,
  And one is for love you know,
  And God put another one in for luck.
  If you search you will find where they grow.

"And you must have hope and you must have faith.
  You must love and be strong, and so
  If you work, if you wait, you will find the place
  Where the four-leaf clovers grow."

It was a sweet, haunting melody that accompanied the words, and the gay party of nine, strolling toward the orchard, hummed it all the way.

There in the shade of the big apple-trees, where

the clover grew in thick patches, they began their search; all together at first, then in little groups of twos and threes, until they had hunted over the entire orchard. Stuart, who had been doing more talking than hunting, went to groping industriously around on his hands and knees, when they all came together again after an hour's search.

"Bradford," he said, emphatically, "I am beginning to think that you and Miss Joyce are right, and that Paradise has a monopoly on the four-leaf kind. I haven't caught a glimpse of one. Not even its shadow."

Lloyd held up a handful. "I found them in several places, thick as hops."

"Which goes to show," he insisted, "that the song, 'If you work, if you wait, you will find the place,' is all a delusion and a snare. You all have worked, and Eugenia and I have waited, and only you, who are 'bawn lucky,' have found any. It's pure luck."

"No," interrupted Miles Bradford, "you can't call strolling around a shady orchard with a pretty girl work, and the song does correspond with the legend. Abdallah worked hard for his first leaf, dug a well with which to bless the thirsty desert for all time. The bit of copper was at the bottom of it. The effort he made for the second almost cost him his life. He rescued a poor slave girl in order to be faithful to a trust imposed in him, and taught her the truths of Allah. The silver leaf was his reward. He found it in the heathen fetish which she gave him in her gratitude. It had been her god.

"I am not sure about the golden leaf, but I think it was the reward of living a wise and honorable life. The day of his birth it was said that he alone wept, while all around him rejoiced; and he resolved to live so well that at the day of his death he should have no cause for tears, and all around him should mourn. No, I'll not have you belittling my hero, Tremont. There was no luck about it whatsoever. He won the first three leaves by unselfish service, faithfulness to every trust, and wise, honorable living, so that he well deserved that Paradise should bring him perfect happiness."

"Girls!" cried Betty, her face lighting up, "*we* must be warm on the trail, with our Tusitala rings, our Warwick Hall motto, and our Order of Hildegarde. A Road of the Loving Heart is as hard to dig in every one's memory as a well in the desert. If we keep the tryst in all things, we're bound to find the silver leaf, and think of the wisdom it takes to weave with the honor of a Hildegarde!"

Eugenia interrupted her: "Oh, Betty, *please* write a legend of the shamrock for girls that will fit modern times. In the old style there are always three brothers or three maidens who start out to find a thing, and only the last one or the youngest one is successful. The others all come to grief. In yours give *everybody* a chance to be happy.

"There is no reason why *every* maiden shouldn't find the leaves according to the Tusitala rings and Ederyn's motto and Hildegarde's yardstick. And then, don't you see, they needn't wait till the end of their lives for the diamond, for *the prince* will bring it! Don't you see? It is his coming that *makes* the perfect happiness!"

Phil laughed. "Stuart's face shows how he appreciates that compliment," he said, "and as for me and all the other sons of Adam, oh, fair layde, I make my bow!" Springing to his feet, he swept her an elaborate curtsey, holding out his coat as if it were the ball-gown of some stately dame in a minuet.

Lloyd, sitting on the grass with her hands clasped on her knees, looked around the circle of smiling faces, and then gave her shoulders a whimsical shrug.

"That's all right if the prince *comes*," she exclaimed. "But how is one to get the diamond leaf if he doesn't? Mammy Eastah told my fortune in a teacup, and she said: 'I see a risin' sun, and a row of lovahs, but I don't see you a-takin' any of 'em, honey. Yo' ways am ways of pleasantness, and all yo' paths is peace, but I'se powahful skeered you'se goin' to be an ole maid. I sholy is, if the teacup signs p'int right.'"

"It will be your own fault, then," answered Phil. "The row of lovers is there in the teacup for you. You've only to take your pick."

"But," began Rob, "maybe it is just as well that she shouldn't choose any of them. The prince's coming doesn't always bring happiness. Look at old Mr. Deckly. For thirty years he and his fair bride have led a regular cat and dog life. And there are the Twicketts and the Graysons and the Blackstones right in this one little valley, to say nothing of all the troubles one reads of in the papers."

"No!" contradicted Eugenia, emphatically. "You have no right to hold them up as examples. It is plainly to be seen that Mrs. Deckly and

Mrs. Twickett and Mrs. Grayson and Mrs. Blackstone were not Hildegardes. They failed to earn their third leaf by doing their weaving wisely. They didn't use their yardsticks. They looked only at the ' village churls,' and wove their webs to fit their unworthy shoulders, so that the men they married were not princes, and they couldn't bring the diamond leaf."

" The name of the prince need not always be *Man,* need it ? " ventured Joyce. " Couldn't it be Success ? It seems to me that if I had struggled along for years, trying to make the most of my little ability, had worked just as faithfully and wisely at my art as I could, it would be perfect happiness to have the world award me the place of a great artist. It would be as much to me as the diamond leaf that marriage could bring. I should think you'd feel that way, too, Betty, about your writing. There are marriages that are failures just as there are artistic and literary careers that are failures, and there are diamond leaves to reward the work and waiting of old maids, just as there are diamond leaves to reward the Hildegardes who use their yardsticks. Sometimes there are girls who don't marry because they sacrifice their lives to taking care of their families, or living for those who are dependent on them. Surely there must be a blessedness and a happiness for them greater than any diamond leaf a prince could bring."

"There is probably," answered Eugenia, "but it seems as if most people of that kind have to wait till they get to Paradise to find it."

"I don't think so," said Betty. "I believe all the dear old-maid aunts and daughters, *who earn the first three leaves,* find the fourth waiting somewhere in this world. It is only the selfish ones, who slight their share of the duties life imposes on every one, who are cross and unlovely and unloved. They probably would not have been happy wives if they had married."

"Well, but what about *me!*" persisted Lloyd. "I nevah expect to have a career, so Success in big lettahs will nevah bring me a medal or a chromo. I am not sacrificing my life for anybody's comfort, and I can nevah have any little nieces and nephews to whom I can be one of those deah old aunts Betty talks about, and there is that dreadful teacup!"

She did not hear Doctor Bradford's laughing answer, for Phil, turning his back on the others, looked down into her upturned face and began to hum, as if to himself, *"From the desert I come to thee!"* Only Mary understood the significance of it as Lloyd did, and she knew why Lloyd suddenly turned away and began passing her hands over the grass around her, as if resuming her search. She wanted to hide her face, into which the color was creeping.

A train whistled somewhere far across the orchard, and Rob took out his watch. The sight of it suggested something in line with the conversation, for when he had noted the time, he touched the spring that opened the back of the case.

"Never you mind, Little Colonel," he said, in a patronizing, big-brotherly tone. "If nobody else will stand between you and that teacup, *I'll* come to the rescue. Bobby won't go back on his old chum. *I'll* bring you a four-leaf clover. Here's one, all ready and waiting."

Lloyd looked across at the watch he held out to her. "Law, Bobby," she exclaimed, giving him the old name she had called him when they first played together, "I supposed you had lost that clovah long ago."

"Not much," he answered. "It's the finest hoodoo ever was. It helped me through high school. I swear I never could have passed in Latin but for your good-luck charm. It's certainly to my interest to hang on to it.

"Think of it, Mary," he added, seeing that her eyes were round with interest, "that was given to me by a princess."

Mary darted a quick look at Lloyd and another one at him to see if he were teasing.

"Oh, I *see!*" she remarked, in a tone of enlightenment.

"What do you see?" he demanded, laughing.

She would not answer, but, ignoring his further attempts to make her talk, she, too, turned again to search for clovers, inwardly excited over the discovery she thought she had made. She would make a note of it in her journal, she decided, something like this: "The plot thickens. The B. M. and Sir F. have a rival they little suspect. R. carries the charm the M. of H. gave him in years gone by, and I can see many reasons why he should be the one to bring her the diamond leaf."

Only two dozen clovers rewarded their united search, but Eugenia was satisfied. "We'll put them in the boxes haphazard," she said, "and the uncertainty of getting one will make it more exciting than if there were one for every box."

The path back to the house led past the kitchen,

where several colored women were helping Aunt
Cindy. Just as they passed, one of them put her
head out of the door to call to a group of children
crowded around one of the windows of the great
house. They were watching the decorators at work
inside the drawing-room, hanging the gate of roses
in the arch. The youngest one was perched on a
barrel that had been dragged up for that purpose,
so that his older brothers and sisters might be
spared the weariness of holding him up to see. A
narrow board laid across the top made an uneasy
and precarious perch for him. He was seated
astride, with his bare black legs dangling down
inside the barrel.

"You M'haley Gibbs," called the woman, "don't
you let Ca'line Allison lean agin that bo'd. It'll
upset Sweety into the bar'l."

Her warning came too late, for even as she called
the slight board was pushed off its foundations by
the weight of the roly-poly Ca'line Allison, and
the pickaninny went down into the barrel as suddenly as a candle is snuffed out by the wind.

"You M'haley, I'll natcherly lay you out,"
shrieked the woman, hurrying up the path to the
rescue. But M'haley, made agile by fifteen years
of constant practice, dodged the cuffing as it was

about to descend, and scuttled around the house to wait till Sweety stopped howling.

"They are Sylvia Gibbs's children," said Lloyd, in answer to Doctor Bradford's astonished comment at seeing so many little negroes in a row. "They can scent a pahty five miles away, and they hang around like little black buzzahds waiting for scraps of the feast. I suppose they feel they have a right to be heah to-day, as Sylvia is helping in the kitchen. They're the same children, Eugenia," she added, "who were heah so much when I had my first house-pahty. M'haley is the one who brought you that awful, skinny, mottled chicken in a bandbox for you to 'take home on the kyers fo' a pet,' she said."

"So she is!" exclaimed Eugenia, as they passed around the corner of the house and caught sight of M'haley, who was peeping out to see if the storm was over, and if it would be safe to return to the sightseeing at the window. Her teeth and eyeballs were ashine with pleasure when Eugenia passed on, after a pleasant greeting and some reference to the chicken. She felt it a great honor to be remembered by the bride, and thanked again, after all these years, for her parting gift. She gave a little giggle when Lloyd came up, and said, with a coy self-conscious air that was extremely amusing to the Northern man, who had never met this type of the race before, " I'se a maid of honah, too, Miss Lloyd."

" You are! " was the surprised answer. " How does that happen? "

" Mammy's gwine to git married agin, to Mistah Robinson, and she says nobody has a bettah right than me to be maid of honah to her own ma's weddin'. So that's how come she toted us all along to you-all's weddin', so that Sweety and Ca'line and the boys could learn how to act at her and Mistah Robinson's."

" When is it to be? " inquired Lloyd.

" To-morrow night. Mammy's done give her fish-fry and ice-cream festible, and she cleahed enough to pay the weddin' expenses. You-all's suah gwine to git an invite, Miss Lloyd."

" It is sort of a benefit," Betty explained to Miles Bradford, as they walked on. " Instead of giving a concert or a recital, the colored people here give a fish-fry and festival whenever they are in need of money. They used to have them just to raise funds for the church, but now it is quite popular for individuals to give them when there is a funeral or a wedding to be paid for. I am so glad

you are going to stay over a few days. We can
show you sights you've never dreamed of in the
North."

Eugenia, first to step into the hall, gave a cry
of pleasure. The florist and his assistants had been
there in their absence, and were just leaving. They
had turned the entire house into a rose-garden.
Hall, drawing-room, and library, and the dining-
room beyond were filled with such lavishness that
it seemed as if June herself had taken possession,
with all her court. Stuart and Eugenia paused
before the tall gate of smilax and American beau-
ties.

"It is the Gate into Paradise, sweetheart," he
whispered, looking through its blossom-covered
bars to the altar beyond, that had been built in the
bay-window of the drawing-room, and covered with
white roses.

"Yes," answered Eugenia, smiling up at him.
"The legend is right. We must enter Paradise to
find the diamond leaf. But I was right, too. It
is my prince who will bring mine to me."

CHAPTER XII.

THE WEDDING

LUNCH was served on the porch, for the tables for the wedding supper were already spread in the dining-room, and Alec had locked the doors that nothing might disturb its perfect order.

"I think we are really going to be able to avoid that last wild rush which usually accompanies home weddings," said Mrs. Sherman, as they sat leisurely talking over the dessert. "Usually the bridesmaids' gloves are missing, or the bride's slippers have been packed into one of the trunks and sent on ahead to the depot. But this time I have tried to have everything so perfectly arranged that the wedding will come to pass as quietly and naturally as a flower opens. I want to have everything give the impression of having *bloomed* into place."

"Eliot and Mom Beck are certainly doing their part to make such an impression," said Eugenia.

" Eliot has already counted over every article I am to wear, a dozen times, and they're all laid out in readiness, even to the 'something blue.' "

" Oh, that reminds me!" began Lloyd, then stopped abruptly. Nobody noticed the exclamation, however, but Mary, and, with swift intuition, she guessed what the something blue had suggested to the maid of honor. It was that bit of turquoise that caused the only scramble in the preparations, for Lloyd could not remember where she had put it.

" I was suah I dropped it into one of the boxes in my top bureau drawer," she said to herself on the way up-stairs. Then, with her finger on her lip, she stopped on the threshold of the sewing-room to consider. She remembered that when she gave up her room to the guests, all the boxes had been taken out of that drawer. Some of them had been put in the sewing-room closet, and some carried to a room at the end of the back hall, where trunks and hampers were stored.

Now, while Betty was down-stairs, helping with a few last details, Lloyd took advantage of her absence to search all the boxes in the closet and drawers of the sewing-room, but the missing turquoise was not in any of them.

"I know I ought to be taking a beauty sleep," she thought, "so I'll be all fresh and fine for the evening, but I must find it, for I promised Phil I'd wear it."

In the general shifting of furniture to accommodate so many guests, several articles had found their way back among the trunks. Among them was an old rocking-chair. It was drawn up to the window now, and, as Lloyd pushed open the door, to her surprise she found Mary Ware half-hidden in its roomy depths. She was tilted back in it with a book in her hands.

Mary was as surprised as Lloyd. She had been so absorbed in the story that she did not hear the knob turn, and as the hinges suddenly creaked, she started half out of her chair.

"Oh!" she exclaimed, settling back when she saw it was only Lloyd. "You frightened me nearly out of my wits. I didn't know that anybody ever came in here." Then she seemed to feel that some explanation of her presence was necessary.

"I came in here because our room is full of clothes, spread out ready to wear. They're all over the room, — mine on one side and Joyce's on the other. I was so afraid I'd forget and flop down on them, or misplace something, that I came in here to read awhile. It makes the afternoon go faster. Seems to me it never will be time to dress."

Lloyd stood looking at the shelves around the room, then said: " If time hangs so heavy on yoah hands, I believe I'll ask you to help me hunt for something I have lost. It's just a trifle, and maybe it is foolish for me to try to find it now, when everything is in such confusion, but it is something that I want especially."

" I'd love to help hunt," exclaimed Mary, putting down her book and holding out her arms to take the boxes which Lloyd was reaching down from the shelves. One by one she piled them on a pack-ing-trunk behind her, and then climbed up beside them, sitting Turk fashion in their midst, and leav-ing the chair by the window for Lloyd.

" It's just a scrap of unset turquoise," explained Lloyd, as she unwrapped a small package, " no larger than one of the beads on this fan-chain. I was in a big hurry when I dropped it into my drawer, and I didn't notice which box I put it in. So we'll have to take out all these ribbons and laces and handkerchiefs and sachet-bags."

It was the first time during her visit that Mary had been entirely alone with her adored Princess, and to be with her now in this intimate way, smoothing her dainty ribbons, peeping into her private boxes, and handling her pretty belongings, gave her a pleasure that was indescribable.

"Shall I open this, too?" she asked, presently, picking up a package wrapped in an old gauze veil.

Lloyd glanced up. "Yes; although I haven't the slightest idea what it can be."

A faint, delicious odor stole out as Mary unwound the veil, an odor of sandalwood, that to her was always suggestive of the "Arabian Nights," of beautiful Oriental things, and of hidden treasures in secret panels of old castles.

"I've hunted for that box high and low!" cried Lloyd, reaching forward to take it. "Mom Beck must have wrapped it so, to keep the dust out of the carving. I nevah thought of looking inside that old veil for anything of any account. I think moah of what it holds than any othah ornament I own."

Mary watched her curiously as she threw back the lid and lifted out a necklace of little Roman pearls. Lloyd dangled it in front of her, lifting the shining string its full length, then letting it slip back into her palm, where it lay a shimmering mass of tiny lustrous spheres. Regarding it intently, she said, with one of those unaccountable impulses which sometimes seize people:

" Mary, I've a great mind to tell you something I've nevah yet told a soul, — how it was I came to make this necklace. I believe I'll weah it when I stand up at the altah with Eugenia. It seems the most appropriate kind of a necklace that a maid of honah could weah."

The story of Ederyn and the king's tryst was fresh in Mary's mind, for Betty had told it at the lunch-table half an hour before, in answer to Doctor Bradford's question about the motto of Warwick Hall; the motto which Betty declared was a surer guide-post to the silver leaf of the magic shamrock than the one Abdallah followed.

" I can't undahstand," began Lloyd, " why I should be telling this to a little thing like you, when I hid it from Betty as if it were a crime. I knew she would think it a beautiful idea, — marking each day with a pearl when its duties had been well done, but I was half-afraid that she would think it conceited of me — conceited for me to count that any of my days were perfect enough to be marked with a pearl. But it wasn't that I thought them so. It was only that I tried my hardest to make the most of them, — in my classes and every way, you know."

As Lloyd went on, telling of the times she had failed and times she had succeeded, Mary felt as if she were listening to the confessions of a white Easter lily. It seemed perfectly justifiable to her that Lloyd should have had tantrums, and stormed at the doctor when he forbade her going back to school after the Christmas vacation, and that she should have cried and moped and made everybody around her miserable for days. Mary's overweening admiration for the Princess carried her to the point of feeling that everybody *ought* to be miserable when she was unhappy. In Mary's opinion it was positively saintly of her the way she took up her rosary again after awhile, trying to string it with tokens of days spent unselfishly at home; days unstained by regrets and tears and idle repinings for what could not be helped.

Mary laughed over the story of one hard-earned pearl, the day spent in making pies and cleaning house for the disagreeable old Mrs. Perkins, who didn't want to be reformed, and who wouldn't stay clean.

" I haven't the faintest idea why I told you all this," said Lloyd at last, once more lifting the string to watch the light shimmer along its lustrous length. "But now you see why I prize this little rosary so highly. It was what lifted me out of my dungeon of disappointment."

Afterward Mary thought of a dozen things she wished she had said to Lloyd while they were there together in the privacy of the trunk-room. She wished she had let her know in some way how much she admired her, and longed to be like her, and how she was going to try all the rest of her life to be a real maid of honor, worthy in every way of her love and confidence. But some shy, unusual feeling of constraint crowded the unspoken words back into her throbbing little throat, and the opportunity passed.

Clasping the pearls around her neck, Lloyd picked up the sandalwood box again and shook it. "Heah's a lot of loose beads of all kinds, with as many colahs as a kaleidoscope. You do bead-work, don't you, Mary? You may have these if you can use them."

In response to her eager acceptance, Lloyd looked around for something to pour the beads into. "There's an empty cologne bottle on that shelf above yoah head. If you will reach it down, I'll poah them into that."

Beads of various sizes and colors, from garnet to amber, poured in a rainbow stream from the box to the wide-necked bottle. Here and there was the glint of cut steel and the gleam of crystal, and several times Mary noticed a little Roman pearl like those on the rosary, and thought with a thrill of the necklace she intended to begin making that very day. Suddenly Lloyd gave an exclamation and reversed the gay-colored stream, pouring it slowly back into the box from the bottle.

"I thought I saw that turquoise," she cried. "I remembah now, it was in my hand when I took off my necklace, and I must have dropped them in heah togethah."

She parted the beads with a cautious forefinger, pushing them aside one at a time. Presently a bit of blue rolled uppermost, and she looked up triumphantly. "There it is!"

Mary flushed guiltily at sight of the turquoise, wondering what Lloyd would think if she knew that she had overheard what Phil had said about that bit of something blue. She went back to her chair and her book by the window after Lloyd left, but the book lay unopened in her lap. She had many things to think of while she slowly turned the bottle between herself and the light and watched its shifting colors. Several times a black bead appeared among the others.

"I'd have had to use black beads more than once," she reflected, "if *I* had been making a rosary, for there's the day I was so rude to Girlie Dinsmore, and the awful time when I got so interested that I eavesdropped."

The wedding was all that Mrs. Sherman had planned, everything falling into place as beautifully and naturally as the unfolding of a flower. The assembled guests seated in the great bower of roses heard a low, soft trembling of harp-strings deepen into chords. Then to this accompaniment two violins began the wedding-march, and the great gate of roses swung wide. As Stuart and his best man entered from a side door and took their places at the altar in front of the old minister, the rest of the bridal party came down the stairs: Betty and Miles Bradford first, Joyce and Rob, then the maid of honor walking alone with her armful of roses. After her came the bride with her hand on her father's arm.

Just at that instant some one outside drew back the shutters in the bay-window, and a flood of late afternoon sunshine streamed across the room, the last golden rays of the perfect June day making a path of light from the gate of roses to the white altar. It shone full across Eugenia's face, down on the long-trained shimmering satin, the little gleaming slippers, the filmy veil that enveloped her, the pearls that glimmered white on her white throat.

Eliot, standing in a corner, nervously watching every movement with twitching lips, relaxed into a smile. "It's a good omen!" she said, half under her breath, then gave a startled glance around to see if any one had heard her speak at such an improper time.

The music grew softer now, so faint and low it seemed the mere shadow of sound. Above the rare sweetness of that undertone of harp and violins rose the words of the ceremony: *"I, Stuart, take thee, Eugenia, to be my wedded wife."*

Mary, standing at her post by the rose gate, felt a queer little chill creep over her. It was so solemn, so very much more solemn than she had imagined it would be. She wondered how she would feel if the time ever came for her to stand in Eugenia's place, and plight her faith to some man in that way — *"for better, for worse, for richer, for poorer, in sickness and in health, until death us do part."*

Eliot was crying softly in her corner now. Yes, getting married was a terribly solemn thing. It didn't end with the ceremony and the pretty clothes and the shower of congratulations. That was only the beginning. *" For better, for worse,"* — that might mean all sorts of trouble and heartache. *" Sickness and death,"* — it meant to be bound all one's life to one person, morning, noon, and night. How very, very careful one would have to be in choosing, — and then suppose one made a mistake and thought the man she was marrying was good and honest and true, and he *wasn't!* It would be all the same, for *" for better, for worse,"* ran the vow, *" until death us do part."*

Then and there, holding fast to the gate of roses, Mary made up her mind that she could never, never screw her courage up to the point of taking the vows Eugenia was taking, as she stood with her hand clasped in Stuart's, and the late sunshine of the sweet June day streaming down on her like a benediction.

" It's lots safer to be an old maid," thought Mary. " I'll take my chances getting the diamond leaf some other way than marrying. Anyhow, if I ever should make a choice, I'll ask somebody else's opinion, like I do when I go shopping, so I'll be sure I'm getting a real prince, and not an imitation one."

It was all over in another moment. Harp and violins burst into the joyful notes of Mendelssohn's march, and Stuart and Eugenia turned from the altar to pass through the rose gate together. Lloyd and Phil followed, then the other attendants in the order of their entrance. On the wide porch, screened and canopied with smilax and roses, a cool green out-of-doors reception-room had been made. Here they stood to receive their guests.

Mary, in all the glory of her pink chiffon dress and satin slippers, stood at the end of the receiving line, feeling that this one experience was well worth the long journey from Arizona. So thoroughly did she delight in her part of the affair, and so heartily did she enter into her duties, that more than one guest passed on, smiling at her evident enjoyment.

" I wish this wedding could last a week," she confided to Lieutenant Logan, when he paused beside her. " Don't you know, they did in the fairy-tales, some of them. There was ' feasting and merrymaking for seventy days and seventy nights.' This one is going by so fast that it will soon be train-time. I don't suppose *they* care," she added, with a nod toward the bride, " for they're going to spend their honeymoon in a Gold of Ophir rose-garden, where there are goldfish in the fountains, and real orange-blossoms. It's out in California, at Mister Stuart's grandfather's. Elsie, his sister, couldn't come, so they're going out to see her, and take her a piece of every kind of cake we have to-night, and a sample of every kind of bonbon. Don't you wonder who'll get the charms in the bride's cake? That's the only reason I am glad the clock is going so fast. It will soon be time to cut the cake, and I'm wild to see who gets the things in it."

The last glow of the sunset was still tinting the sky with a tender pink when they were summoned to the dining-room, but indoors it had grown so dim that a hundred rose-colored candles had been lighted. Again the music of harp and violins floated through the rose-scented rooms. As Mary glanced around at the festive scene, the tables gleaming with silver and cut glass, the beautiful costumes, the smiling faces, a line from her old school reader kept running through her mind: *" And all went merry as a marriage-bell! And all went merry as a marriage-bell!"*

It repeated itself over and over, through all the gay murmur of voices as the supper went on, through the flowery speech of the old Colonel when he stood to propose a toast, through the happy tinkle of laughter when Stuart responded, through the thrilling moment when at last the bride rose to cut the mammoth cake. In her nervous excitement, Mary actually began to chant the line aloud, as the first slice was lifted from the great silver salver: " All went merry — " Then she clapped her hand over her mouth, but nobody had noticed, for Allison had drawn the wedding-ring, and a chorus of laughing congratulations was drowning out every other sound.

As the cake passed on from guest to guest, Betty cried out that she had found the thimble. Then Lloyd held up the crystal charm, the one the bride had said was doubly lucky, because it held imbedded in its centre a four-leaved clover. Nearly every slice had been crumbled as soon as it was taken, in search of a hidden token, but Mary, who had not dared to hope that she might draw one, began leisurely eating her share. Suddenly her teeth met on something hard and flat, and glancing down, she saw the edge of a coin protruding from the scrap of cake she held.

" Oh, it's the shilling! " she exclaimed, in such open-mouthed astonishment that every one laughed,

and for the next few moments she was the centre
of the congratulations. Eugenia took a narrow
white ribbon from one of the dream-cake boxes,
and passed it through the hole in the shilling, so
that she could hang it around her neck.

" Destined to great wealth!" said Rob, with
mock solemnity. " I always did think I'd like to
marry an heiress. I'll wait for you, Mary."

" No," interrupted Phil, laughing, " fate has
decreed that I should be the lucky man. Don't you
see that it is Philip's head with Mary's on that
shilling? "

" Whew!" teased Kitty. " Two proposals in
one evening, Mary. See what the charm has done
for you already! "

Mary knew that they were joking, but she turned
the color of her dress, and sat twiddling the coin
between her thumb and finger, too embarrassed to
look up. They sat so long at the table that it was
almost train-time when Eugenia went up-stairs to
put on her travelling-dress. She made a pretty
picture, pausing midway up the stairs in her bridal
array, the veil thrown back, and her happy face
looking down on the girls gathered below. Leaning far over the banister with the bridal bouquet in
her hands, she called:

" Now look, ye pretty maidens, standing all a-row,
   The one who catches this, the next bouquet shall throw."

There was a laughing scramble and a dozen
hands were outstretched to receive it. " Oh, Joyce
caught it! Joyce caught it!" cried Mary, dancing
up and down on the tips of her toes, and clapping
her hands over her mouth to stifle the squeal of
delight that had almost escaped. " Now, some day
I can be maid of honor."

" So that's why you are so happy over your
sister's good fortune, is it?" asked Phil, bent on
teasing her every time opportunity offered.

" No," was the indignant answer. " That is
some of the reason, but I'm gladdest because she
didn't get left out of everything. She didn't get
one of the cake charms, so I hoped she would catch
the bouquet."

When the carriage drove away at last, a row of
shiny black faces was lined up each side of the
avenue. All the Gibbs children were there, and
Aunt Cindy's other grandchildren, with their hands
full of rice.

" Speed 'em well, chillun!" called old Cindy.
waving her apron. The rice fell in showers on the
top of the departing carriage, and two little white
slippers were sent flying along after it, with such

force that they nearly struck Eliot, sitting beside
the coachman. Tired as she was, she turned to
smile approval, for the slippers were a good omen,
too, in her opinion, and she was happy to think that
everything about her Miss Eugenia's wedding had
been carried out properly, down to this last pro-
pitious detail.

As the slippers struck the ground, quick as a cat,
M'haley darted forward to grab them. "Them
slippahs is mates!" she announced, gleefully, "and
I'm goin' to tote 'em home for we-all's wedding.
I kain't squeeze into 'em myself, but Ca'line Allison
suah kin."

Once more, and for the last time, Eugenia leaned
out of the carriage to look back at the dear faces
she was leaving. But there was no sadness in the
farewell. Her prince was beside her, and the Gold
of Ophir rose-garden lay ahead.

CHAPTER XIII.

DREAMS AND WARNINGS

" It's all ovah now!" exclaimed Lloyd, stifling a yawn and looking around the deserted drawing-room, where the candles burned low in their sconces, and the faded roses were dropping their petals on the floor. Mr. Forbes and Doctor Tremont had just driven away to catch the midnight express for New York, and the last guest but Rob had departed.

" It's all over with that gown of yours, too, isn't it?" asked Phil, glancing at the airy pink skirt, down whose entire front breadth ran a wide, zig-zag rent. " It's too bad, for it's the most becoming one I've seen you wear yet. I'm sorry it must be retired from public life so early in its career."

Lloyd drew the edges of the largest holes together. " Yes, it's ruined beyond all hope, for I stepped cleah through it when I tripped on the stairs, and it pulled apart in at least a dozen places, just as a thin veil would. But you'll see it again, and on anothah maid of honah. M'haley nevah waited to see if I was hurt, but pounced on it and began to beg for it befoah I got my breath again. She said she could fix it good enough for her to weah to her mammy's wedding. She would ' turn it hine side befo' ' and tie her big blue sash ovah it. Imagine! She'll be heah at the break of day to get it."

"Do you know it is almost that time now?" asked Betty, coming in from the dining-room with seven little heart-shaped boxes. "Here's our cake, and godmother says we'd better take it and go to dreaming on it soon, or the sun will be up before we get started."

"Now remembah," warned Lloyd, as Rob slipped his box into his pocket and began looking around for his hat, "we have all promised to tell our dreams to each othah in the mawning. We'll wait for you, so come ovah early. Come to breakfast."

"Thanks. I'll be on hand all right. I'll probably have to wake the rest of you."

"Don't you do it!" exclaimed Phil. "I'll warn you now, if you're waking, *don't* call me early, mother, dear. If you do, to-morrow won't be the happiest day of all *your* glad New Year. I'll promise you that. How about you, Bradford?"

"Oh, I'm thinking of sitting up all night," he answered, laughing, "to escape having any dreams. Miss Mary assures me they will come true, and one might have a nightmare after such a spread as that wedding-supper. I can hardly afford to take such risks."

A moment after, Rob's whistle sounded cheerfully down the avenue and Alec was going around the house, putting out the down-stairs lights. Late as it was, when they reached their room, Joyce stopped to smooth every wrinkle out of her bridesmaid dress, and spread it out carefully in the tray of her trunk.

"It is so beautiful," she said, as she plumped the sleeves into shape with tissue-paper. "As long as an accident had to happen to one of us it was lucky that it was Lloyd's dress that was torn. She has so many she wouldn't wear it often anyhow, and this will be my best evening gown all summer. I expect to get lots of good out of it at the seashore."

"I'm glad it wasn't mine that was torn," responded Mary, following Joyce's example and folding hers away also, with many loving pats. "Probably there'll be a good many times I can wear it

here this summer, but there'll never be a chance on the desert, and I shall have outgrown it by next summer, so when I go home I'm going to lay it away in rose-leaves with these darling little satin slippers, because I've had the best time of my life in them. In the morning Betty and I are going to pick all the faded roses to pieces and save the petals. Eugenia wants to fill a rose-jar with part of them. Betty knows how to make that potpourri that Lloyd's Grandmother Amanthis always kept in the rose-jars in the drawing-room. She's copied the receipt for me.

" I'm not a bit sleepy," she continued. " I've had such a beautiful time I could lie awake all the rest of the night thinking about it. Maybe it's because I drank coffee when I'm not used to it that I'm so wide awake, and I ate — *oh, how I ate!*"

One by one the up-stairs lights went out, and a deep silence fell on the old mansion. The ticking of the great clock on the stairs was the only sound. The serene peace of the starlit night settled over The Locusts like brooding wings. The clock struck one, then two, and the long hand was half-way around its face again before any other sound but the musical chime broke the stillness. Then a succession of strangled moans began to penetrate the consciousness of even the soundest sleeper. Whoever it was that was trying to call for help was evidently terrified, and the terror of the cries sent a cold chill through every one who heard them.

"It's burglars," shrieked Lloyd, sitting up in bed. "Papa Jack! They're in Joyce's room! They're trying to strangle her! Papa Jack!"

Lights glimmered in every room, and doors flew open along the hall. A dishevelled little group in bath-robes and pajamas rushed out, Mr. Sherman with a revolver, Miles Bradford with a heavy Indian club, and Phil with his walking-stick with the electric battery in its head. He flashed it like a search-light up and down the hall.

At the first moan, Joyce had wakened, and realizing that it came from Mary's corner of the room, began to grope on the table beside her bed for matches. Her fingers trembled so she could scarcely muster strength to scratch the match when she found it. Then she glanced across the room and began to laugh hysterically.

"It's all right!" she called. "Nobody's killed! Mary's just having a nightmare!"

By this time Mr. Sherman had opened the door, and the blinding glare of Phil's electric light flashed full in Mary's eyes. At the same instant Lloyd opened the door on the other side, between the two rooms, and Betty and Mrs. Sherman followed her in. So when Mary struggled back to wakefulness far enough to sit up and look around in a dazed way, the room seemed full of people and lights and voices, and she tried to ask what had happened. She was still sobbing and trembling.

" What's the matter, Mary?" called Phil from the hall. " Were the Indians after you again?"

" Oh, it was awfuller than Indians," wailed Mary, in a shrill, excited voice. " It was the worst nightmare I ever had! I can't shake it off. I'm scared yet."

" Tell us about it," said Mrs. Sherman, soothingly. " That's the best remedy, for the terror always evaporates in the telling, and makes one wonder how anything foolish could have seemed frightful."

" I — was being married," wailed Mary, " to a man I couldn't see. And just as soon as it was over he turned from the altar and said, ' *Now* we'll begin to lead a cat and dog life.' And, oh, it was so awful," she continued, sobbingly, the terror of the dream still holding her, " he — he *barked* at me! And he showed his teeth, and I had to spit and mew and hump my back whether I wanted to or not."

Her voice grew higher and more excited with every sentence. "And I could feel my claws growing longer and longer, and I knew I'd never have fingers again, only just paws with fur on 'em! Ugh! It made me sick to feel the fur growing over me that way. I cried and cried. Now as I tell about it, it begins to sound silly, but it was awful then, — so dark, and me hanging by my claws to the edge of the wood-shed roof, ready to drop off. I thought Phil was in the house, and I tried to call him, but I couldn't remember his name. I got mixed up with the Philip on the shilling, and I kept yelling, Shill! Philling! Shilling! and I couldn't make him understand. He wouldn't come!"

As she picked up the corner of the sheet to wipe her eyes Mrs. Sherman and the girls burst out laughing, and there was an echoing peal of amusement in the hall. The affair would not have seemed half so ridiculous in the daylight, but to be called out of bed at that hour to listen to such a dream, told only as Mary Ware could tell it, impressed the entire family as one of the funniest things that had ever happened. They laughed till the tears came.

"I don't see what ever put such a silly thing into my head," said Mary, finally, beginning to feel mortified as she realized what an excitement she had created for nothing.

"It was Rob's talking about people who live a regular cat and dog life," said Betty. "Don't you remember how long we talked about it to-day down in the clover-patch?"

"You mean yesterday," prompted Phil from the hall, "for it's nearly morning now. And, Mary, I'll tell you why you had it. It's a warning! A solemn warning! It means that you must never, never marry."

"That's what I thought, too," quavered Mary, so seriously that they all laughed again.

"I hope everybody will excuse me for waking them up," called Mary, as they began to disperse to their rooms. "Oh, dear!" she added to Joyce, as she lay back once more on her pillow. "Why is it that I am always doing such mortifying things! I am *so* ashamed of myself."

The lights went out again, and after a few final giggles from Lloyd and Betty, silence settled once more over the house. But the terror of the nightmare had taken such hold upon Mary that she could not close her eyes.

"Joyce," she whispered, "do you mind if I come

over into your bed? I'm nearly paralyzed, I'm so scared again."

Slipping across the floor as soon as Joyce had given a sleepy consent, Mary crept in beside her sister in the narrow bed, and lay so still she scarcely breathed, for fear of disturbing her. Presently she reached out and gently clasped the end of Joyce's long plait of hair. It was comforting to be so near her. But even that failed to convince her entirely that the dream was a thing of imagination. It seemed so real, that several times before she fell asleep she laid her hands against her face to make sure that her fingers had not developed claws, and that no fur had started to grow on them.

The dreams told around the breakfast-table next morning seemed tame in comparison to Mary's recital the night before. Rob had had none at all, which was interpreted to mean that he would live and die an old bachelor. Miles Bradford had a dim recollection of being in an automobile with a girl who seemed to be a sort of a human kaleidoscope, for her face changed as the dream progressed, until she had looked like every woman he ever knew. They could think of no interpretation for that dream. Lloyd's was fully as indefinite.

" I thought I was making a cake," she said, " and

there was a big bowl of eggs on the table. But every time I started to break one Mom Beck would say, 'Don't do that, honey. Don't you see it is somebody's haid?' And suah enough, every egg I took up had somebody's face on it, like those painted Eastah eggs; Rob's, and Phil's, and Malcolm's, and Doctah Bradford's, and evah so many I'd nevah seen befoah."

"A very appropriate dream for a Queen of Hearts," said Phil, "and anybody can see it's only a repetition of Mammy Easter's fortune, the 'row of lovahs in the teacup.' Tell us which one you are going to choose."

"It's Joyce's turn," was the only answer Lloyd would make.

"And my dream was positively brilliant," replied Joyce. "I thought we were all at The Beeches, and Allison, and Kitty, and all of us were making Limericks. Kitty began:

> "'There was a lieutenant named Logan,
> Who found one day a small brogan.'

Then she stuck, and couldn't get any farther, and Allison had to be smart and pun on my name. She made up a line:

> "'So what will Joyce Ware if she meets a great bear?'

Nobody could get the last rhyme for awhile, but after floundering around a few minutes I had a sudden inspiration and sprang up and struck an attitude as if I were on the stage, and solemnly thundered out:

" ' And how can he shoot him with *no* gun ? '

" In my dream it seemed the most thrilling thing — I was the heroine of the hour, and Lieutenant Logan took me aside and told me that the question which I had embodied in that last line was the question of the ages. It had staggered the philosophers and scientists of all times. Nobody could answer that question — ' how can he shoot him with *no* gun,' and he was a better and a happier man, to think that I had rhymed that ringing query with the proud name of Logan. It's the silliest dream I ever had, but you can't imagine how real it seemed at the time. I was so stuck up over his compliments that I began flouncing around with my head held high, like the picture of ' Oh, fie! you haughty Jane.' "

" Oh, Joyce, what a dream to dream on wedding-cake!" exclaimed Mary, with a long indrawn breath. There was no mistaking her interpretation of it. Everybody laughed, and Joyce hastened to explain, " It isn't worth anything, Mary. It'll never come true, for just before I came down-stairs to breakfast I discovered my little box of cake lying on the table under a pile of ribbons. It had been there all night. I had forgotten to put it under my pillow. And," she added, cutting short Mary's exclamation of disappointment, " *your* box lay beside it. We both were so busy putting away our dresses, and talking over the wedding that we forgot the most important thing of all."

" Well, I'm certainly glad that mine wasn't under my head when I had that dreadful nightmare! " exclaimed Mary, in such a relieved tone that every one laughed again. " I couldn't help taking it as a warning."

" Joyce and I must have changed places in our sleep," said Betty, when her turn came. " She was making verses, and I was trying to draw. But I did my drawing with a thimble. I thought some one said, ' Betty always likes to put her finger in everybody's pie, and now she has a fate thimble to wear on it, she'll mix up things worse than ever.' And I said, ' No, I'll be very conservative, and only make a diagram of the way the animals should go into the ark, and then let them do as they please about following my diagram.' So I began to draw with the thimble on my finger, but instead of animals going into the ark they were people going over Tanglewood stile into the churchyard, and then into the church — a great procession of people in the funniest combinations. There was old Doctor Shelby and the minister's great-aunt, Allison and Lieutenant Stanley, Kitty and Doctor Bradford, Lloyd and Rob, and dozens and dozens besides."

" Lloyd and Rob," echoed the Little Colonel, her face dimpling. " Think of that, Bobby! You nevah in yoah wildest dreams thought of that combination, now did you? "

" No, I never did," confessed Rob, with an amused smile. " Betty has just put it into my head. She is like the old woman who told her children not to put beans in their ears while she was gone. They never would have dreamed of doing such a thing if she hadn't suggested it, but, of course, they wanted to see how it would feel, and immediately proceeded to fill their ears with beans as soon as her back was turned."

" You can profit by their example," laughed Lloyd. " They found that it hurt. It would have been bettah if they had paid no attention to her suggestion."

" Moral," added Rob, " don't do it. Betty,

don't you dare put any more dangerous notions in my head."

Phil's turn came next. " My dream is soon told," he said. " I had been sleeping like the dead — a perfectly dreamless sleep — till Mary woke us up with her cat-fight. That aroused me so thoroughly that I didn't go to sleep again for more than an hour. Then when I did drop off at nearly morning, I dreamed that there was a spider on my head, and I gave it a tremendous whack to kill it. It was no dream whack, I can tell you, but a real live double-fisted one, that made me see stars. It actually made a dent in my cranium and got me so wide awake that I couldn't drop off again. I got up and sat by the window till there were faint streaks of light in the sky. I did the rest of my dreaming with my eyes open, so I don't have to tell what it was about."

" I can guess," thought Mary, intercepting the swift glance he stole across the table at something blue. This time it was the ribbon that tied Lloyd's hair, a big bow of turquoise taffeta, knotted becomingly at the back of her neck. Lloyd, unconscious of the glance, had turned to speak to Miles Bradford, to answer his question about Sylvia Gibbs's wedding.

" Yes, it really is to take place to-night in the colohed church. M'haley was heah befoah we were awake, to get the dress and to repeat the invitation for the whole family to attend. There are evah so many white folks invited, M'haley says. All the Waltons and MacIntyres, of co'se, because Miss Allison is their patron saint, and they swear by her, and all the families for whom Sylvia has washed."

" It is extremely fortunate for those of us who are going away so soon that she set the date as early as to-night," said Doctor Bradford. " Twenty-four hours later would have cut us out."

Phil interrupted him. " Don't bring up such disagreeable topics at the table, Bradford. It takes my appetite to think that we have only one more day in the Valley — that it has come down to a matter of a few hours before we must begin our farewells."

" Speaking of farewells," said Rob, " who-all's coming down to the station with me to wave good-by to Miss Bonham? She goes back to Lexington this morning."

" We'll all go," answered Lloyd, promptly. " Mothah will be glad to get us out of the way while the servants give the place a grand ' aftah the ball ' cleaning, and Joyce wants to see the girls once moah befoah she begins packing, to arrange several things about their journey."

" How does it happen that Logan and Stanley are not going with Miss Bonham? " asked Rob. " Isn't their time up, too, or can't they tear themselves away? "

" I thought you knew," answered Joyce. " Miss Allison arranged it all last night. You know she goes up to Prout's Neck, in Maine, for awhile every summer, and this year Allison and Kitty are going with her. She has offered to take me under her wing all the way, and has arranged her route to go right past the place where the summer art school is, on Cape Cod coast. Lieutenant Logan and Lieutenant Stanley are staying over a day longer than they had intended, in order to go part of the way with us, and Phil and Doctor Bradford are leaving a day earlier to take advantage of such good company all the way home. Won't it be jolly, — eight of us! Kitty calls it a regular house-party on wheels."

" I certainly envy you," answered Rob. " Miss Allison is the best chaperone that can be imagined, just like a girl herself; and Allison and Kitty are as good as a circus any day. I'll wager it didn't take much persuading to make Stanley stay over.

He hasn't eyes for anything or anybody but Allison."

"He had eyes for Bernice Howe the night of Katie Mallard's musicale," said Betty. "He scarcely left her."

"Do you know why?" asked Rob in an aside. They were rising from the table now, strolling out to the chairs and hammocks on the shady porch. He spoke in a low tone as he walked along beside her.

"It is very ungallant for me to say such a thing, but between you and me and the gate-post, Betty, he was roped into being so attentive. Bernice Howe beats any girl I ever saw for making dates with fellows, and handling her cards so as to make it seem she is immensely popular. It is an old trick of hers, and that night it was very apparent what she was trying to do. Alex Shelby was there, you remember, and when she saw him talking to Lloyd every chance he got, she didn't want it to appear that she was being neglected by the man who had brought her, and with a little skilful manœuvring she managed to bag the lieutenant's attention. I've been wanting to ask you for some time, why is it that she seems so down on the Little Colonel?"

"She isn't!" declared Betty, much surprised.

" You must be letting your imagination run away with you, Rob. There isn't a girl in the Valley friendlier and sweeter to Lloyd than Bernice Howe. You watch them next time they are together, and see. They've been good friends for years."

" Then all I can say is that some girls have a queer idea of friendship. It's downright *catty* the way they purr and rub around to your face, and then show their spiteful little claws when your back is turned. That's what I've noticed Bernice doing lately. She calls her all the sugary names in the dictionary when she's with her, but when her back is turned — well, it's just a shrug of the shoulders or a lift of the eyebrows or a little twist of the mouth maybe, but they insinuate volumes. What makes girls do that way, Betty? Boys don't. If they have any grievance they fight it out and then let each other alone."

" I'm sure I don't know why," answered Betty. " I'll be honest with you and confess that you are right. Half the girls at school were that way. They might be fair and high-minded about everything else, but when it came to that one thing they were — well, as you say, regular cats. They didn't have the faintest conception of what a David and Jonathan friendship could be like. Even the ordinary kind didn't seem to bind them in any way, or impose any obligation on them when their own interests were concerned."

" Deliver me from such friends!" ejaculated Rob. " I'd rather have a sworn enemy. He wouldn't do me half the harm." Then after a pause, " I suppose, if you haven't noticed it, then Lloyd hasn't either, that Bernice is bitterly jealous of her."

" No, I am sure she has not."

" Then I wish you'd drop her a hint. I couldn't mention the subject to her, because it is an old fight of ours. You know how we've squabbled for hours over it — the difference between the codes of honor in a girl's friendships and boys'. No matter how carefully I made the distinction that I meant the average girl, and not all of them, she always flared into a temper, and in order to be loyal to her entire sex, took up arms against me in a regular pitched battle. She's ordered me off the place more than once, and yet in her soul I believe she agrees with me."

" But, Rob, if that is a pet theory of yours that you go around applying in a wholesale way, isn't it barely possible that you've made a mistake this time and imagined that Bernice is two-faced in her friendship ? "

Rob shook his head. " She'll be at the station this morning. You can see for yourself, if you keep your eyes open."

" Now, to be explicit, just what is it I shall see? " retorted Betty. But Phil interrupted their tête-à-tête at that point, and when they started to the station an hour later, her question was still unanswered. Bernice Howe was there, as Rob had predicted, and Katie Mallard and several other of the Valley girls who had enjoyed the hospitality of The Beeches during Miss Bonham's visit.

" It looks quite like a garden-party," said Miles Bradford to Miss Allison, watching the pretty girls, in their light summer costumes, flutter around the waiting-room. " I don't know whether to compare them to a flock of butterflies or a bouquet of sweet peas. I am glad we are going to take some of them with us to-morrow, and wish — "

Betty, who had turned to listen, because his smiling glance seemed to include her in the conversation, failed to hear what it was he wished. Bernice Howe, who was standing with her back to her, took occasion just then to draw Miss Bonham aside, and her voice, although pitched in a low key, was unusually penetrating. At the same moment the entire party shifted positions to make room for some new arrivals in the waiting-room, and Betty was jostled so that she was obliged to dodge a corpulent woman with a carpet-bag and a lunch-basket. When she recovered her balance she found herself out of range of Doctor Bradford's voice, but almost touching elbows with Bernice. She was saying:

"We're going to miss you dreadfully, Miss Bonham. I always do miss Allison's guests and Kitty's nearly as much as my own. They're so dear about sharing them with me. Now some girls are so stingy, they fairly keep their visitors under lock and key — that is, if they are men. They wouldn't dream of taking them to call on another girl. Afraid to, I suppose. Afraid of losing their own laurels. There's one of the kind."

Betty saw her nod with a meaning smile toward Lloyd, and caught another sentence or two in which the words, "Queen of Hearts, tied to her apron-string," gave her the drift of the remarks.

"She's plainly trying to give Miss Bonham an unpleasant impression of Lloyd to carry away with her," thought Betty. "She's hurt because she wasn't invited to the coon hunt, and the other little affairs we had for the bridal party. She never took it into consideration that what would have been perfectly convenient at another time was out of the question when the house was so full of guests and all torn up with preparations for the wedding. Lloyd had all she could do then to think of the guests in the house, without considering those outside. It certainly is a flimsy sort of a friendship that can't overlook a seeming neglect like that or make due allowances. Besides, if she feels slighted, why doesn't she keep it to herself, and not try to get even by giving Miss Bonham a false impression of her? Rob is right. Boys don't stoop to such mean little things. In the first place they don't magnify trifles into big grievances, and go around feeling slighted and hurt over nothing."

"Here comes the train!" called Ranald, seizing Miss Bonham's suit-case and leading the way to the door. There was a moment of hurried good-byes, a fluttering of handkerchiefs, a waving of hats. Then the train passed on, leaving the group gazing after it.

"What are we going to do now?" asked Rob. "Will you all come over to the store and have some peanuts?"

"No, you're all coming up home with me," said Lloyd, "Miss Allison and everybody. I saw Alec carrying some watahmelons into the ice-house, and they'll be good and cold by this time. We'll cut them out on the lawn."

Ranald excused himself, saying he had promised to take his Aunt Allison to the dressmaker's in the pony-cart, but Allison and Kitty promptly accepted the invitation for themselves and the two lieutenants. Katie Mallard walked on with one and Joyce the other, Rob and Betty bringing up the rear. Lloyd still waited.

"Come on, Bernice," she urged. "The watah-melons are mighty fine, and we'd love to have you come."

"No, dearie," was the reply. "I've a lot of things to do to-day, but I'll see you to-night at the darky wedding."

"I'm mighty sorry you can't come," called Lloyd, then hurried on to catch up with the others. As she joined Rob and Betty she felt intuitively they had changed their subject of conversation at her approach. She had caught the question, "Then are you going to warn her?" and Betty's reply, "What's the use? It would only make her feel bad."

"What's that about warnings?" asked Lloyd, catching Betty's hand and swinging it as she walked along beside her.

" Something that Betty doesn't believe in," began Rob, " just as I don't believe in dreams. Why wouldn't Bernice come with you? "

" She said she had so much to do. Mistah Shelby is coming out latah. He is going to take her to Sylvia's wedding to-night."

" Speaking of warnings," burst out Rob, impulsively, " I'm going to give you one, Lloyd, whether you like it or not. Don't be too smiling and gracious when you meet Alex Shelby, or Bernice will be assaulting you for poaching on her preserves. You must keep out of her bailiwick if you want to keep her friendship. It's the kind that won't stand much of a strain."

" What do you mean, Rob Moore? " demanded Lloyd, hesitating between a laugh and the old feeling of anger that always flashed up when he referred to girls' friendships in that superior tone.

" I am devoted to Bernice and she is to me. If you are trying to pick a quarrel you may as well go along home, for I'm positively not going to fuss with you about anything whatsoevah until aftah all the company is gone."

" No'm! I don't want to quarrel," responded Rob, with exaggerated meekness. " I was merely giving you a warning — sort of playing Banshee for your benefit, but you don't seem to appreciate my efforts. Let's talk about watermelons."

CHAPTER XIV.

A SECOND MAID OF HONOR

IT was a new experience to Miles Bradford, this trudging through the dense beech woods on a summer night behind a row of flickering lanterns. The path they followed was a wide one, and well worn by the feet of churchgoing negroes, for it was the shortest cut between the Valley and Stumptown, a little group of cabins clustered around the colored church.

Ranald led the way with a brakeman's lantern, and Rob occasionally illuminated the scene by electric flashes from the head of the walking-stick he was flourishing. A varied string of fiery dragons, winged fish, and heathen hobgoblins danced along beside them, for Kitty was putting candles in a row of Japanese lanterns when they arrived at The Beeches, and nearly everybody in the party accepted her invitation to take one. Mary chose a sea-serpent with a grinning face, and Elise a pretty oval one with birds and cherry blossoms on each side.

Lloyd did not take any. Her hands were already filled with a huge bouquet of red roses.

"Sylvia asked me to carry these," she explained to Miles Bradford, "and to weah a white dress and this hat with the red roses on it. Because I was maid of honah at Eugenia's wedding she seems to think I can reflect some sawt of glory on hers. She said she wanted all her young ladies to weah white."

"Who are her young ladies, and why?" he asked.

"Allison, Kitty, Betty, and I. You see, Sylvia's grandfathah was the MacIntyre's coachman befoah the wah, and her mothah is our old Aunt Cindy. She considahs that she belongs to us and we belong to her."

Farther down the line they could hear Katie Mallard's cheerful giggle as she tripped over a beech root, then Bernice Howe's laugh as they all went slipping and sliding down a steep place in the path which led to the hollow crossed by the dry creek bed.

"Sing!" called Miss Allison, who was chaperoning the party, and picking her way behind the others with Mary and Elise each clinging to an arm. "There's such a pretty echo down in this

hollow. Listen!" The tune that she started was
one of the popular songs of the summer. It was
caught up by every one in the procession except
Miles Bradford, and he kept silent in order to enjoy
this novel pilgrimage to the fullest. The dark
woods rang with the sweet chorus, and the long
line of fantastic lanterns sent weird shadows bob-
bing up in their wake.

The bare, unpainted little church had just been
lighted when they arrived, and a strong smell of
coal-oil and smoking wicks greeted them.

"It's too bad we are so early," said Miss Allison. "Sylvia would have preferred us to come in
with grand effect at the last moment, but I'm too
tired to wait for the bridal party. Let's put our
lanterns in the vestibule and go in and find
seats."

A pompous mulatto man in white cotton gloves
and with a cluster of tuberoses in his buttonhole ushered the party down the aisle to the seats of honor
reserved for the white folks. There were seventeen
in the party, too many to sit comfortably on the
two benches, so a chair was brought for Miss Allison. After the grown people were seated, each of
the little girls managed to squeeze in at the end of
the seats nearest the aisle. Lloyd found herself

seated between Mary Ware and Alex Shelby. Leaning forward to look along the bench, she found that Bernice came next in order to Alex, then Lieutenant Stanley and Allison, Doctor Bradford and Betty.

She had merely said good evening to Alex Shelby when they met at The Beeches, and, although positions in the procession through the woods had shifted constantly, it had happened she had not been near enough to talk with him. Now, with only Mary Ware to claim her attention, they naturally fell into conversaton. It was only in whispers, for the audience was assembling rapidly, and the usher had opened the organ in token that the service was about to begin.

There had been an attempt to decorate for the occasion. Friends of the bride had resurrected both the Christmas and Easter mottoes, so that the wall behind the pulpit bore in tall, white cotton letters, on a background of cedar, the words, "Peace on Earth, Good Will to Men." Fresh cedar had been substituted for the yellowed branches left over from the previous Christmas, and fresh diamond dust sprinkled over the grimy cotton to give it its pristine sparkle of Yule-tide frost.

"An appropriate motto for a wedding," whispered Alex Shelby to Lloyd. Only his eyes laughed. His face was as solemn as the usher's own as he turned to gaze at the word "Welcome" over the door, and the fringe of paper Easter lilies draping the top of each uncurtained window.

Bernice claimed his attention several moments, then he turned to Lloyd again. "Do tell me, Miss Lloyd," he begged, "what is that wonderfully and fearfully made thing in the front of the pulpit? Is it a doorway or a giant picture-frame? And what part is it to play in the ceremony?"

Lloyd's face dimpled, and an amused smile flashed up at him from the corner of her eye. Then she lowered her long lashes demurely, and seemed to be engrossed with her bunch of roses as she answered him.

"The coquettish thing!" thought Bernice, seeing the glance but not hearing the whisper which followed it.

"Sh! Don't make me laugh! Everybody is watching to see if the white folks are making fun of things, and I'm actually afraid to look up again for feah I'll giggle. Maybe it's a copy of Eugenia's gate of roses. It looks like the frame of a doahway. Just the casing, you know. Maybe it's a doah of mawning-glories they're going to pass through. I recognize those flowahs twined all around it. We made them a long time ago for the lamp-shades when the King's Daughtahs had an oystah suppah at the manse. I made all those purple mawning-glories and Betty made the yellow ones."

Glancing over his shoulder, he happened to spy a familiar face behind him, the kindly old black face of his uncle's cook.

" Howdy, Aunt Jane!" he exclaimed, with a friendly smile. Then, in a stage whisper, he asked, " Aunt Jane, can you tell me? Are those morning-glories artificial?"

The old woman wrinkled her face into a knot as she peered in the direction of the pulpit, toward which he nodded. One of the words in his question puzzled her. It was a stranger to her. But, after an instant, the wrinkles cleared and her face broadened into a smile.

" No'm, Mistah Alex. Them ain't artificial flowahs, honey. They's made of papah."

Again an amused smile stole out of the corner of Lloyd's eye to answer the gleam of mischief in Alex's. Not for anything would she have Aunt Jane think that she was laughing, so her eyes were bent demurely on her roses again. Again Bernice, leaning forward, intercepted the glance and misinterpreted it. When Alex turned to her to repeat Aunt Jane's explanation, she barely smiled, then relapsed into sulky silence. Finding several other attempts at conversation received with only monosyllables, he concluded that she was not in a mood to talk, and naturally turned again to Lloyd.

He had not been out in the Valley for years, he told her. The last visit he had made to his uncle, old Doctor Shelby, had been the summer that the Shermans had come back to Lloydsboro from New York. He remembered passing her one day on the road. She had squeezed through a hole in the fence between two broken palings, and was trying to pull a little dog through after her; a shaggy Scotch and Skye terrier.

" That was my deah old Fritz," she answered, " and I was probably running away. I did it every chance I had."

" The next time I saw you," he continued, " I was driving along with uncle. I was standing between his knees, I remember, proud as a peacock because he was letting me hold the reins. I was just out of kilts, so it was a great honor to be trusted with the lines. When we passed your grandfather on his horse, he had you up in front of his saddle, and uncle called out, 'Good morning, little Colonel.'"

These reminiscences pleased Lloyd. It flattered her to think he remembered these early meetings so many years ago. His relationship to the old doctor whom she loved as her own uncle put him on a very friendly footing.

The church filled rapidly, and by the time the seats were crowded and people were jostling each other to find standing-room around the door, a young colored girl in a ruffled yellow dress seated herself at the organ. First she pulled out all the stops, then adjusting a pair of eyeglasses, opened a book of organ exercises. Then she felt her sash in the back, settled her side-combs, and raising herself from the organ bench, smoothed her skirts into proper folds under her. After these preliminaries she leaned back, raised both hands with a grand flourish, and swooped down on the keys.

"Bang on the low notes and twiddle on the high!" laughed Lloyd, under her breath. "Listen, Mistah Shelby. She's playing the same chord in the bass straight through."

"Is that what makes the fearsome discord?" he asked. "It makes me think of an epitaph I once

saw carved on a pretentious headstone in a little
village cemetery:

> " ' Here lies one
> Who never let her left hand know
> What her right hand done.' "

" Neithah of Laura's hands will evah find out
what the othah one is trying to do," whispered
Lloyd. " She is supposed to be playing the wed-
ding-march. Hark! There is a familiah note:
' *Heah comes the bride.*' They must be at the doah.
Well, I wish you'd look!"

Every head was turned, for the bridal party was
advancing. Slowly down the aisle came M'haley,
in the pink chiffon gown from Paris. Mom Beck's
quick needle had altered it considerably, for in some
unaccountable way the slim bodice fashioned to fit
Lloyd's slender figure, now fastened around M'haley's waist without undue strain. The skirt, though
turned " hine side befo'," fell as skirts should fall,
for the fulness had been shifted to the proper
places, and the broad sky-blue sash covered the
mended holes in the breadth Lloyd had torn on the
stairs.

With her head high, and her armful of flowers
held in precisely the same position in which Lloyd

had carried hers, she swept down the aisle in such exact imitation of the other maid of honor, that every one who had seen the first wedding was convulsed, and Kitty's whisper about " Lloyd's understudy " was passed with stifled giggles from one to another down both benches.

Ca'line Allison came next, in a white dress and the white slippers that had been thrown after Eugenia's carriage with the rice.

She was flower girl, and carried an elaborate fancy basket filled with field daisies. A wreath of the same snowy blossoms crowned her woolly pate, and an expression of anxiety drew her little black face into a distressed pucker. She had been told that at every third step she must throw a handful of daisies in the path of the on-coming bride, and her effort to keep count and at the same time keep her balance on the high French heels was almost too much for her.

During her many rehearsals M'haley had counted her steps for her: " One, two, three — *throw!* One, two, three — *throw!* " She had gone through her part every time without mistake, for her feet were untrammelled then, and her flat yellow soles struck the ground in safety and with rhythmic precision. She could give her entire mind to the graceful scattering of her posies. But now she walked as if she were mounted on stilts, and her way led over thin ice. The knowledge that she must keep her own count was disconcerting, for she could not " count in her haid," as M'haley had ordered her to do. She was obliged to whisper the numbers loud enough for herself to hear. So with her forehead drawn into an anxious pucker, and her lips moving, she started down the aisle whispering, " One, two, three — *throw!* One, two, three — *throw!* " Each time, as she reached the word " throw " and grasped a handful of daisies to suit the action to the word, she tilted forward on the high French heels and almost came to a full stop in her effort to regain her balance.

But Ca'line Allison was a plucky little body, accustomed to walking the tops of fences and cooning out on the limbs of high trees, so she reached the altar without mishap. Then with a loud sigh of relief she settled her crown of daisies and rolled her big eyes around to watch the majestic approach of her mother.

No matron of the four hundred could have swept down the aisle with a grander air than Sylvia. The handsome lavender satin skirt she wore had once trailed its way through one of the most elegant re-

ceptions ever given in New York, and afterward
had graced several Louisville functions. Its owner
had given Sylvia the bodice also, but no amount of
stretching could make it meet around Sylvia's ample
figure, so the proceeds of the fish-fry and ice-cream
festival had been invested in a ready-made silk
waist. It was not the same shade of lavender as the
skirt, but a gorgeous silver tissue belt blinded one
to such differences. The long kid gloves, almost
dazzling in their whiteness, were new, the fan borrowed, and the touch of something blue was furnished by a broad back-comb of blue enamel sur-
mounted by rhinestones. One white glove rested
airily on " Mistah Robinson's " coat-sleeve, the other
carried a half-furled fan edged with white feathers.

M'haley and Ca'line Allison waited at the altar,
but the bridal couple, turning to the right, circled
around it and mounted the steps leading up into
the pulpit. The mystery of the wooden frame was
explained now. It was not a symbolical doorway
through which they were to pass, but a huge flower-
draped picture-frame in which they took their
places, facing the congregation like two life-sized
portraits in charcoal.

The minister, standing meekly below them between M'haley and Ca'line Allison, with his back to

"'ONE, TWO, THREE — *THROW!*'"

the congregation, prefaced the ceremony by a long and flowery discourse on matrimony, so that there was ample time for the spectators to feast their eyes on every detail of the picture before them. Except for a slight stir now and then as some neck was craned in a different position for a better view, the silence was profound, until the benediction was pronounced.

At the signal of a blast from the wheezy organ the couple, slowly turning, descended the steps. Ca'line Allison, in her haste to reach the aisle ahead of them to begin her posy-throwing again, nearly tilted forward on her nose. But with a little crow-hop she righted herself and began her spasmodic whispering, " One, two, three — *throw!* "

After the couple came M'haley and the pompous young minister. Then Lloyd, who had caught the bride's smile of gratification as her eyes rested on the white dress and red roses of this guest of honor, and who read the appealing glance that seemed to beckon her, rose and stepped into line. The rest of Sylvia's young ladies immediately followed, and the congregation waited until all the rest of the white folks passed out, before crowding to the carriage to congratulate " Brothah and Sistah Robinson."

Lloyd went on to the carriage to speak to Sylvia

and give her the armful of roses to decorate the wedding-feast, before joining the others, who were lighting the lanterns for their homeward walk.

" You'd better come in the light of ours, Miss Lloyd," said Alex Shelby, coming up to her with Bernice beside him. " We might as well take the lead. Ranald seems to be having trouble with his wick."

Lloyd hesitated, remembering Rob's warning, but glancing behind her, she saw Phil hurrying toward her, and abruptly decided to accept his invitation. She knew that Phil was trying to arrange to walk home with her. This would be his last opportunity to walk with her, and while she knew that he would respect her promise to her father enough not to infringe on it by talking openly of his regard for her, his constant hints and allusions would keep her uncomfortable. He seemed to take it for granted that she was bound to come around to this point of view some day, and regard him as the one the stars had destined for her.

So it was merely to escape a tête-à-tête with Phil which made her walk along beside Alex, and put out a hand to draw Mary Ware to the other side. She linked arms with her as they pushed through the crowd, and started down the road four abreast.

But the fences were lined with buggies and wagons, and the scraping wheels and backing horses kept them constantly separating and dodging back and forth across the road, more often singly than in pairs.

By the time they reached the gap in the fence where the path through the woods began, the others had caught up with them, and they all scrambled through in a bunch. Lloyd looked around, and, with a sensation of relief, saw that Kitty had Phil safely in tow. She would be free as far as The Beeches, at any rate. At a call from Elise, Mary ran back to join her. Positions were being constantly shifted on the homeward way, just as they had been before, and, looking around, Lloyd decided that she would slip back presently with some of the others, who would not think that two is company and three a crowd, as Bernice might be doing. The backward glance nearly caused her a fall, for a big root in the path made her ankle turn, and Alex Shelby's quick grasp of her elbow was all that saved her.

" It was my fault, Miss Lloyd," he insisted. " I should have held the lantern differently. There, I'll go slightly ahead and light the path better. Can you see all right, Bernice? "

"Yes," she answered, shortly, out of humor that he should be as careful of Lloyd's comfort as her own. She trudged along, taking no part in the conversation. It was a general one, extending all along the line, for Rob at the tail and Ranald at the head shouted jokes and questions back and forth like end-men at a minstrel show. Laughing allusions to the maid of honor and Ca'line Allison were bandied back and forth, and when the line grew unusually straggling, Kitty would bring them into step with her, "One, two, three — *throw!*"

Neither Lloyd nor Alex noticed the determined silence in which Bernice stalked along, and when she presently slipped back with the excuse that she wanted to speak to Katie, they scarcely missed her. There was nothing unusual in the action, as all the others were changing company at intervals. At the entrance-gate to The Beeches she joined them again, for her nearest road home led through the Walton place, and they were to part company here with Lloyd and her guests.

For a few minutes there was a babel of good-nights and parting sallies, in the midst of which Alex Shelby managed to say to Lloyd in a low tone, "Miss Lloyd, I am coming out to the Valley again a week from to-day. If you haven't any engagement for the afternoon will you go horseback-riding with me?"

The consciousness that Bernice had heard the invitation and was displeased, confused her so that for a moment she lost her usual ease of manner. She wanted to go, and there was no reason why she should not accept, but all she could manage to stammer was an embarrassed, "Why, yes — I suppose so." But the next instant recovering herself, she added, graciously, "Yes, Mistah Shelby, I'll be glad to go."

"Come on, Lloyd," urged Betty, swinging her hand to pull her into the group now drawn up on the side of the road ready to start. They had made their adieux.

"All right," she answered, locking arms with Betty. "Good night, Mistah Shelby. Good night, Bernice."

He acknowledged her nod with a courteous lifting of his hat, and repeated her salutation. But Bernice, standing stiff and angry in the starlight, turned on her heel without a response.

"What on earth do you suppose is the mattah with Bernice?" exclaimed Lloyd, in amazement, as they turned into the white road leading toward home.

CHAPTER XV.

WITH the desire to make this last walk together as pleasant as possible, Lloyd immediately put Bernice out of her mind as far as she was able. But she could not rid herself entirely of the recollection that something disagreeable had happened. The impression bore down on her like a heavy cloud, and was a damper on her high spirits. Outwardly she was as gay as ever, and when the walk was over, led the party on a foraging expedition to the pantry.

Rob and Phil were almost unroarious in their merriment now, and, as they devoured cold baked ham, pickles, cheese, beaten biscuit, and cake, they had a fencing-match with carving-knives, and gave a ridiculous parody of the balcony scene in " Romeo and Juliet." Mary, looking on with a sandwich in each hand, almost choked with laughter, although she, too, was borne down by the same feeling that depressed Lloyd, of something very disagreeable having happened.

She had been so ruffled in spirit all the way home that she had lagged behind the others, and it was only when Rob and Phil began their irresistible foolishness that she had forgotten her grievance long enough to laugh. No sooner had they all gone up-stairs, and she was alone with Joyce, than her indignation waxed red-hot again, and she sputtered out the whole story to her sister.

"And," she said, in conclusion, "that hateful Bernice Howe said the meanest things to Katie. Elise and I were walking just behind, and we couldn't help hearing. She said that Lloyd had deliberately set to work to flirt with Mr. Shelby, and get him to pay her attention, and that, if Katie would watch, she'd soon see how it would be. He'd be going to see Lloyd all the time instead of her."

"Sh!" warned Joyce. "They'll hear you all over the house. Your voice is getting higher and higher."

Her warning came too late. Already several sentences had penetrated into the next room, and a quick knock at the door was followed by the entrance of Lloyd, looking as red and excited as Mary.

"Tell me what it was, Mary," she demanded. "What made Bernice act so? I was sure you knew from the way you looked when you joined us."

Mary was almost in tears as she repeated what she had told Joyce, for she could see that the Little Colonel's temper was rising to white heat.

"And Bernice said it wasn't the first time you had treated her so. She said that Malcolm Mac-Intyre was so attentive to her last summer while you were away at the Springs; that he sent her flowers and candy and took her driving, and was like her very shadow until you came home. Then he dropped her like a hot potato, and you monop-olized him so that you succeeded in keeping him away from her altogether."

"Malcolm!" gasped Lloyd. "Malcolm was my especial friend long befoah I evah heard of Bernice Howe! Why, at the very first Valentine pahty I evah went to, he gave me the little silvah arrow he won in the archery contest, for me to remembah him by. I've got it on this very minute."

She put her hand up to the little silver pin that fastened the lace of her surplice collar. "Malcolm *always has* called himself my devoted knight, and he — "

She paused. There were some things she could

not repeat; that scene on the churchyard stile the winter day they went for Christmas greens, when he had begged her for a talisman, and his low-spoken reply, "I'll be whatever you want me to be, Lloyd." There were other times, too, of which she could not speak. The night of the tableaux was the last one, when she had strolled down the moonlighted paths with him at The Beeches, and he had insisted that it was the "glad morrow" by his calendar, and time for her Sir Feal to tell her many things, especially as he was going away for the rest of the summer on a long yachting trip, and somebody else might tell her the same things in his absence. So many years she had taken his devotion as a matter of course, that it provoked her beyond measure to have Bernice insinuate that she had angled for it.

Lloyd knew girls who did such things; who delighted in proving that they had a superior power of attraction, and who would not scruple to use all sorts of mean little underhand ways to lessen a man's admiration for some other girl, and appropriate it for themselves. She had even heard some of the girls at school boast of such things.

"For pity's sake, Lloyd!" one of them had said, "don't look at me that way. 'All's fair in love and war,' and a girl's title to popularity is based on the number of scalp-locks she takes."

Lloyd had despised her for that speech, and now to have Bernice openly say that she was capable of such an action was more than she could endure calmly. She set her teeth together hard, and gripped the little fan she still happened to be carrying, as if it were some live thing she was trying to strangle.

"And she said," Mary added, slowly, reluctant to add fuel to the flame, yet unable to withstand the impelling force of Lloyd's eyes, which demanded the whole truth, "she said that she had been sure for some time that Mr. Shelby was just on the verge of proposing to her, and that, if you succeeded in playing the same game with him that you did with Malcolm, she'd get even with you if it took her till her dying day. Then, right on top of that, you know, she heard him ask if you'd go horseback riding with him. So that's why she was so angry she wouldn't bid you good night."

Lloyd's clenched hand tightened its grasp on the fan till the delicate sticks crunched against each other. She was breathing so hard that the little arrow on her dress rose and fell rapidly. The silence was so intense that Mary was frightened.

She did not know what kind of an outburst to expect. All of a sudden, taking the fan in both hands, Lloyd snapped it in two, and then breaking the pieces into a hundred splinters, threw them across the room into the open fireplace. She stood with her back to the girls a moment, then, to Mary's unspeakable astonishment, forced herself to speak as calmly as if nothing had happened, asking Joyce some commonplace question about her packing. There was a book she wanted her to slip into her trunk to read at the seashore. She was afraid it would be forgotten if left till next day, so she went to her room to get it.

As the door closed behind her, Mary turned to Joyce in amazement. " I don't see how it was possible for her to get over her temper so quickly," she exclaimed. " The change almost took my breath."

" She isn't over it," answered Joyce. " She simply got it under control, and it will smoulder a long time before it's finally burnt out. She's dreadfully hurt, for she and Bernice have been friends so long that she is really fond of her. Nothing hurts like being misunderstood and misconstrued in that way. It is the last thing in the world that *Lloyd* would do — suspect a friend of mean motives. From what I've seen of Bernice, she is an uncomfortable sort of a friend to have; one of the sensitive, suspicious kind that's always going around with her feelings stuck out for somebody to tread on. She's always looking for slights, and when she doesn't get real ones, she imagines them, which is just as bad."

If Lloyd's anger burned next morning, there was no trace of it either in face or manner, and she made that last day one long to be remembered by her departing guests.

"How lonesome it's going to be aftah you all leave," she said to Joyce. "The rest of the summah will be a stupid anticlimax. The house-pahty and the wedding should have come at the last end of vacation instead of the first, then we would have had something to look forward to all summah, and could have plunged into school directly aftah it."

"This July and August will be the quietest we have ever known at The Locusts," chimed in Betty. "Allison and Kitty leave to-night with you all, Malcolm and Keith are already gone, and Rob will be here only a few days longer. That's the last straw, to have Rob go."

"What's that about yours truly?" asked Rob,

coming out of the house and beginning to fan himself with his hat as he dropped down on the porch
step.

"I was just saying that we shall miss you so
much this summer. That you're always our
stand-by. It's Rob who gets up the rides and
picnics, and comes over and stirs us out of our
laziness by making us go fishing and walking and
tennis-playing. I'm afraid we'll simply go into
our shells and stay there after you go."

"Ah, ha! You do me proud," he answered, with
a mocking sweep of his hat. "'Tis sweet to be
valued at one's true worth. Don't think for a
moment that I would leave you to pine on the stem
if I could have my own way. But I'm my mother's
angel baby-boy. She and daddy think that grandfather's health demands a change of air, and they
are loath to leave me behind. So, unwilling to
deprive them of the apple of their several eyes, I
have generously consented to accompany them.
But you needn't pine for company," he added, with
a mischievous glance at Lloyd. "Alex Shelby
expects to spend most of the summer with the old
doctor, and he'll be a brother to you all, if you'll
allow it."

Lloyd made no answer, so he proceeded to make

several more teasing remarks about Alex, not knowing what had taken place before. He even ventured to repeat the warning about her keeping within her own bailiwick, as Bernice's friendship was not the kind that could stand much strain.

To his surprise Lloyd made no answer, but, setting her lips together angrily, rose and went into the house, her head high and her cheeks flushed.

"Whew!" he exclaimed, with a soft whistle. "What hornet's nest have I stirred up now?"

Joyce and Betty exchanged glances, each waiting for the other to make the explanation. Then Joyce asked: "Didn't you see the way Bernice snubbed her last night at the gate, when we left The Beeches?"

"Nary a snub did I see. It must have happened when I was groping around in the path for something that I had flipped out of my pocket with my handkerchief. It rang on the ground like a piece of money, and I feared me I had lost one of me ducats. What did she do?"

"I can't tell you now," said Joyce, hurriedly, lowering her voice. "Here come Phil and Doctor Bradford."

"No matter," he answered, airily. "I have no curiosity whatsoever. It's a trait of character en-

tirely lacking in my make-up." Then he motioned
toward Mary, who was sitting in a hammock, cutting the pages of a new magazine. " Does *she*
know ? "

Joyce nodded, and feeling that they meant her,
Mary looked up inquiringly. Rob beckoned to her
ingratiatingly.

" Come into the garden, Maud," he said in a low
tone. " I would have speech with thee."

Laughing at his foolishness, but in a flutter of
pleasure, Mary sprang up to follow him to the
rustic seat midway down the avenue. As Joyce's
parting glance had not forbidden it, she was soon
answering his questions to the best of her ability.

" You see," he explained, " it's not out of curiosity that I ask all this. It's simply as a means of
precaution. I can't keep myself out of hot water
unless I know how the land lies."

That last day of the house-party seemed the
shortest of all. Betty and Miles Bradford strolled
over to Tanglewood and sat for more than an hour
on the shady stile leading into the churchyard.
Lloyd and Phil went for a last horseback ride, and
Mary, watching them canter off together down the
avenue, wondered curiously if he would have any-

thing more to say about the bit of turquoise and all it stood for.

As she followed Joyce up-stairs to help her pack her trunk, a little wave of homesickness swept over her. Not that she wanted to go back to the Wigwam, but to have Joyce go away without her was like parting with the last anchor which held her to her family. It gave her a lonely set-adrift feeling to be left behind. She took her sister's parting injunctions and advice with a meekness that verged so nearly on tears that Joyce hastened to change the subject.

"Think of all the things I'll have to tell you about when I get back from the seashore. Only two short months, — just eight little weeks, — but I'm going to crowd them so full of glorious hard work that I'll accomplish wonders. There'll be no end of good times, too: clambakes and fishing and bathing to fill up the chinks in the days, and the story-telling in the evenings around the driftwood fires. It will be over before we know it, and I'll be back here ready to take you home before you have time to really miss me."

Cheered by Joyce's view of the subject, Mary turned her back a moment till she had winked away the tears that had begun to gather, then straightway started out to make the most of the eight little weeks left to her at The Locusts. When she went with the others to the station " to give the house-party on wheels a grand send-off," as Kitty expressed it, her bright little face was so happy that it brought a smiling response from every departing guest.

" Good-by, Miss Mary," Miles Bradford said, cordially, coming up to her in the waiting-room. " The Pilgrim Father has much to thank you for. You have helped him to store up some very pleasant memories of this happy Valley."

" Good-by, little Vicar," said Phil next, seizing both her hands. " Think of the Best Man whenever you look at the Philip on your shilling, and think of his parting words. *Do* profit by that dreadful dream, and don't take any rash steps that would lead to another cat-fight. We'll take care of your sister," he added, as Mary turned to Joyce and threw her arms around her neck for one last kiss.

" Lieutenant Logan will watch out for her as far as he goes, and I'll keep my eagle eye on her the rest of the way."

" Who'll keep an eagle eye on you? " retorted Mary, following them out to the platform.

He made a laughing grimace over his shoulder, as he turned to help Joyce up the steps.

"What a good time they are going to have together," thought Mary, watching the group as they stood on the rear platform of the last car, waving good-by. "And what a different parting this is from that other one on the desert when he went away with such a sorry look in his eyes." He was facing the future eagerly this time, strong in hope and purpose, and she answered the last wave of his hat with a flap of her handkerchief, which seemed to carry with it all the loyal good wishes that shone in her beaming little face.

Miles Bradford had made a hurried trip to the city that morning, to attend to a matter of business, going in on the ten o'clock trolley and coming back in time for lunch. On his return, he laid a package in Mary's lap, and handed one to each of the other girls. Joyce's was a pile of new July magazines to read on the train. Lloyd's was a copy of "Abdallah, or the Four-leaved Shamrock," which had led to so much discussion the morning of the wedding, when they hunted clovers for the dream-cake boxes.

Mary's eyes grew round with surprise and delight when she opened her package and found inside the white paper and gilt cord a big box of Huyler's candies. " With the compliments of the Pilgrim Father," was pencilled on the engraved card stuck under the string.

There was layer after layer of chocolate creams and caramels, marshmallows and candied violets, burnt almonds and nougat, besides a score of other things — specimens of the confectioner's art for which she knew no name. She had seen the outside of such boxes in the show-cases in Phœnix, but never before had such a tempting display met her eyes as these delicious sweets in their trimmings of lace paper and tinfoil and ribbons, crowned by a pair of little gilt tongs, with which one might make dainty choice.

Betty's gift was not so sightly. It looked like an old dried sponge, for it was only a ball of matted roots. But she held it up with an exclamation of pleasure. " Oh, it is one of those fern-balls we were talking about this morning! I've been wanting one all year. You see," she explained to Mary, when she had finished thanking Doctor Bradford, " you hang it up in a window and keep it wet, and it turns into a perfect little hanging garden, so fine and green and feathery it's fit for fairyland. It will grow as long as you remember to water it. Gay Melville had one last year in her window at school, and I envied her every time I saw it."

" Now what does that make me think of? " said Mary, screwing up her forehead into a network of wrinkles and squinting her eyes half-shut in her effort to remember. " Oh, I know! It's something I read in a paper a few days ago. It's in China or Japan, I don't know which, but in one of those heathen countries. When a young man wants to find out if a girl really likes him, he goes to her house early in the dawn, and leaves a growing plant on the balcony for her. If she spurns him, she tears it up by the roots and throws it out in the street to wither, and I believe breaks the pot; but if she likes him, she takes it in and keeps it green, to show that he lives in her memory."

A shout of laughter from Rob and Phil had made her turn to stare at them uneasily. " What are you laughing at? " she asked, innocently. " I *did* read it. I can show you the paper it is in, and I thought it was a right bright way for a person to find out what he wanted to know without asking."

It was very evident that she hadn't the remotest idea she had said anything personal, and her ignorance of the cause of their mirth made her speech all the funnier. Doctor Bradford laughed, too, as he said with a formal bow: "I hope you will take the suggestion to heart, Miss Betty, and let my memory and the fern-ball grow green together."

Then, Mary, realizing what she had said when it was too late to unsay it, clapped her hands over her mouth and groaned. Apologies could only make the matter worse, so she tried to hide her confusion by passing around the box of candy. It passed around so many times during the course of the afternoon that the box was almost empty by train-time. Mary returned to it with unabated interest after the guests were gone. It was the first box of candy she had ever owned, and she wondered if she would ever have another.

"I believe I'll save it for a keepsake box," she thought, gathering it up in her arms to follow Betty up-stairs. Rob had come back with them from the station, and, taking the story of "Abdallah," he and Lloyd had gone to the library to read it together.

Betty was going to her room to put the fern-ball to soak, according to directions. Feeling just a trifle lonely since her parting from Joyce, Mary wandered off to the room that seemed to miss her, too, now that all her personal belongings had disappeared from wardrobe and dressing-table. But she was soon absorbed in arranging her keepsake box. Emptying the few remaining scraps of candy into a paper bag, she smoothed out the lace paper, the ribbons, and the tinfoil to save to show to Hazel Lee. These she put in her trunk, but the gilt tongs seemed worthy of a place in the box. The Pilgrim Father's card was dropped in beside it, then the heart-shaped dream-cake box, holding one of the white icing roses that had ornamented the bride's cake. Last and most precious was the silver shilling, which she polished carefully with her chamois-skin pen-wiper before putting away.

"I don't need to look at *you* to make me think of the Best Man," she said to the Philip on the coin. "There's more things than you that remind me of him. I certainly would like to know what sort of a fate you are going to bring me. There's about as much chance of my being an heiress as there is of that nightmare coming true."

CHAPTER XVI.

THE GOLDEN LEAF OF HONOR

IT was a compliment that changed the entire course of Mary's summer; a compliment which Betty gleefully repeated to her, imitating the old Colonel's very tone, as he gesticulated emphatically to Mr. Sherman:

"I tell you, Jack, she's the most remarkable child of her age I ever met. It is wonderful the information she has managed to pick up in that God-forsaken desert country. I say to you, sir, she can tell you as much now about scientific bee-culture as any naturalist you ever knew. Actually quoted Huber to me the other day, and Maeterlinck's 'Life of the Bee!' Think of a fourteen-year-old girl quoting Maeterlinck! With the proper direction in her reading, she need never see the inside of a college, for her gift of observation amounts to a talent, and she har it in her to make herself not only an honor to her sex, but one of the most interesting women of her generation."

Mary looked up in blank amazement when Betty danced into the library, hat in hand, and repeated what the old Colonel had just said in her hearing. Compliments were rare in Mary's experience, and this one, coming from the scholarly old gentleman of whom she stood in awe, agitated her so much that three successive times she ran her needle into her finger, instead of through the bead she was trying to impale on its point. The last time it pricked so sharply that she gave a nervous jerk and upset the entire box of beads on the floor.

" See how stuck-up that made me," she said, with an embarrassed laugh, shaking a tiny drop of blood from her finger before dropping on her knees to grope for the beads, which were rolling all over the polished floor. " It's so seldom I hear a compliment that I haven't learned to take them gracefully."

" Godmother is waiting in the carriage for me," said Betty, pinning on her hat as she spoke, " or I'd help you pick them up. I just hurried in to tell you while it was fresh in my mind, and I could remember the exact words. I had no idea it would upset you so," she added, mischievously.

Left to herself, Mary soon gathered the beads back into the box and resumed her task. She was making a pair of moccasins for Girlie Dinsmore's doll. Her conscience still troubled her for playing stork, and she had resolved to spend some of her abundant leisure in making amends in this way. But only her fingers took up the same work that had occupied her before Betty's interruption. Her thoughts started off in an entirely different direction.

A most romantic little day-dream had been keeping pace with her bead-stringing. A day-dream through which walked a prince with eyes like Rob's and a voice like Phil's, and the wealth of a Crœsus in his pockets. And he wrote sonnets to her and called her his ladye fair, and gave her not only one turquoise, but a bracelet-ful.

Now every vestige of sentiment was gone, and she was sitting up straight and eager, repeating the old Colonel's words. They were making her unspeakably happy. " She has it in her to make herself not only an honor to her sex, but one of the most interesting women of her generation." " To make herself an honor," — why, that would be winning the third leaf of the magic shamrock — the *golden* one! Betty had said that she believed that every one who earned those first three leaves was sure to find the fourth one waiting somewhere in the world. It wouldn't make any difference then whether she was an old maid or not. She need not be dependent on any prince to bring her the diamond leaf, and that was a good thing, for down in her heart she had her doubts about one ever coming to her. She loved to make up foolish little day-dreams about them, but it would be too late for him to come when she was a grandmother, and she wouldn't be beautiful till then, so she really had no reason to expect one. It would be much safer for her to depend on herself, and earn the first three in plain, practical ways.

"To make herself an honor." The words repeated themselves again and again, as she rapidly outlined an arrow-head on the tiny moccasin in amber and blue. Suddenly she threw down the needle and the bit of kid and sprang to her feet. "*I'll do it!*" she said aloud.

As she took a step forward, all a-tingle with a new ambition and a firm resolve, she came face to face with her reflection in one of the polished glass doors of the bookcase. The intent eagerness of its gaze seemed to challenge her. She lifted her head as if the victory were already won, and confronted the reflection squarely. "I'll do it!" she said, solemnly to the resolute eyes in the glass door. "You see if I don't!"

Only that morning she had given a complacent glance to the long shelves of fiction, with which she expected to while away the rest of the summer. There would be other pleasant things, she knew, drives with Mrs. Sherman, long tramps with the girls, and many good times with Elise Walton; but there would still be left hours and hours for her to spend in the library, going from one to another of the famous novelists, like a bee in a flower garden.

"With the proper direction in her reading," the old Colonel had said, and Mary knew without telling that she would not find the proper beginning among the books of fiction. Instinctively she felt she must turn to the volumes telling of real people and real achievements. Biographies, journals, lives, and letters of women who had been, as the Colonel said, an honor to their sex and the most interesting of their generation. She wished that she dared ask him to choose the first book for her, but she hadn't the courage to venture that far. So she chose at random.

"Lives of Famous Women" was the volume that happened to attract her first, a collection of short sketches. She took it from the shelf and glanced through it, scanning a page here and there, for she was a rapid reader. Then, finding that it bade fair to be entertaining, down she dropped on the rug, and began at the preface. Lunch stopped her for awhile, but, thoroughly interested, she carried the book up to her room and immediately began to read again.

When she went down to the porch before dinner that evening, she did not say to herself in so many words that maybe the Colonel would notice what she was reading, but it was with the hope that he would that she carried the book with her. He did notice, and commended her for it, but threw her into a flutter of confusion by asking her what similarity she had noticed in the lives of those women she was reading about.

It mortified her to be obliged to confess that she had not discovered any, and she thought, as she nervously fingered the pages and looked down at her toes, " That's what I got for trying to appear smarter than I really am."

" This is what I meant," he began, in his didactic way. " Each of them made a specialty of some one thing, and devoted all her energies to accomplishing that purpose, whether it was the establishing of a salon, the discovery of a star, or the founding of a college. They hit the bull's-eye, because they aimed at no other spot on the target. I have no patience with this modern way of a girl's taking up a dozen fads at a time. It makes her a jack-at-all-trades and a master of none."

The Colonel was growing eloquent on one of his favorite topics now, and presently Mary found him giving her the very guidance she had longed for. He was helping her to a choice. By the time dinner was announced, he had awakened two ambitions within her, although he was not conscious of the fact himself. One was to study the strange insect life of the desert, in which she was already deeply interested, to unlock its treasures, unearth its secrets, and add to the knowledge the world had already amassed, until she should become a recognized authority on the subject. The other was to prove by her own achievements the truth of something which the Colonel quoted from Emerson. It flattered her that he should quote Emerson to her, a mere child, as if she were one of his peers, and she wished that Joyce could have been there to hear it.

This was the sentence: *"If a man can write a better book, preach a better sermon, or make a bet-*

ter mouse-trap than his neighbor, though he build his house in the woods, the world will make a beaten track to his door."

Mary did not yet know whether the desert would yield her the material for a book or a mouse-trap, but she determined that no matter what she undertook, she would force the world to " make a beaten track to her door." The first step was to find out how much had already been discovered by the great naturalists who had gone before her, in order that she might take a step beyond them. With that in view, she plunged into the course of study that the Colonel outlined for her with the same energy and dogged determination which made her a successful killer of snakes.

Lloyd came upon her the third morning after the breaking up of the house-party, sitting in the middle of the library floor, surrounded by encyclopædias and natural histories. She was verifying in the books all that she had learned by herself in the desert of the habits of trap-door spiders, and she was so absorbed in her task that she did not look up.

Lloyd slipped out of the room without disturbing her, wishing she could plunge into some study as absorbing, — something that would take her mind from the thoughts which had nagged her like a persistent mosquito for the last few days. She knew that she had done nothing to give Bernice just cause for taking offence, and it hurt her to be misunderstood.

" If it were anything else," she mused, as she strolled up and down under the locusts, " I could go to her and explain. But explanation is impossible in a case of this kind. It would sound too conceited for anything for me to tell her what I know to be the truth about Malcolm's attentions to her, and as for the othah — " she shrugged her shoulders. " It would be hopeless to try that. Oh, if I could only talk it ovah with mothah or Papa Jack! " she sighed.

But they had gone away immediately after the house-party, for a week's outing in the Tennessee mountains. She could have gone to her grandfather for advice on most questions, but this was too intangible for her to explain to him. Betty, too, was as much puzzled as herself.

" I declare," she said, when appealed to, " I don't know what to tell you, Lloyd. It's going to be such a dull summer with everybody gone, and Alex Shelby is so nice in every way, it does seem unfair for you to have to put such a desirable companionship from you just on account of another girl's jealousy. On the other hand, Bernice is an old playmate, and you can't very well ignore the claims of such a long-time friendship. She has misjudged and misrepresented you, and the opportunity is yours, if you will take it, to show her how mistaken she is in your character."

Now, as Lloyd reached the end of the avenue and stopped in front of the gate, her face brightened. Katie Mallard was hurrying down the railroad track, waving her parasol to attract her attention.

" I can't come in," she called, as she came within speaking distance. " I'm out delivering the most informal of invitations to the most informal of garden-parties to-morrow afternoon. I want you and Betty to help receive."

" Who else is going to help?" asked Lloyd, when she had cordially accepted the invitation for herself and Betty.

" Nobody. I had intended to have Bernice Howe, and went up there awhile ago to ask her. She said maybe she'd come, but she certainly wouldn't help receive if you were going to. She's dreadfully down on you, Lloyd."

" Yes, I know it. I've heard some of the catty

things she said about my breaking up the friendship between her and Malcolm. It's simply absurd,
and it makes me so boiling mad every time I think
about it that I feel like a smouldering volcano.
There aren't any words strong enough to relieve
my mind. I'd like to thundah and lighten at her."

" Yes, it is absurd," agreed Katie. " I told her so
too. I told her that Malcolm always had thought
more of you than any girl in the Valley, and always
would. And she said, well, you had no ' auld lang
syne ' claim on Alex, and that if he once got started
to going to Locust you'd soon have him under your
thumb as you do every one else, and that would be
the end of the affair for her."

" As if I were an old spidah, weaving webs for
everybody that comes along! " cried Lloyd, indignantly. " She's no right to talk that way."

" I think it's because she really cares so much,
and not that she does it to be spiteful," said Katie.
" She hasn't a bit of pride about hiding her feeling for him. She openly cried about it while she
was talking to me."

" What do you think I ought to do? " asked
Lloyd, with a troubled face. " I like Mistah Shelby
evah so much, and I'd like to be nice to him for the
old doctah's sake if for no othah reason, for I'm

devoted to *him*. And I really would enjoy seeing him often, especially now when everybody else is gone or going for the rest of the summah. Besides, he'd think it mighty queah for me to write to him not to come next Thursday. But I'd hate to really interfere with Bernice's happiness, if it has grown to be such a serious affair with her that she can cry about it. I'd hate to have her going through the rest of her life thinking that I had deliberately wronged her, and if she's breaking her heart ovah it " — she stopped abruptly.

" Oh, I don't see that you have any call to do the grand renouncing act! " exclaimed Katie. " Why should you cut yourself off from a good time and a good friend by snubbing him? It will put you in a very unpleasant light, for you couldn't explain without making Bernice appear a perfect ninny. And if you don't explain, what will he think of you? Let me tell you, it is more than she would do for you if you were in her place. Somehow, with us girls, life seems like a game of ' Hold fast all I give you.' What falls into your hands is yours by right of the game, and you've no call to hand it over to the next girl because she whimpers that she wants to be ' it.' Don't you worry. Go on and have a good time."

With that parting advice Katie hurried away, and Lloyd was left to pace up and down the avenue more undecided than before. It was late in the afternoon of the next day when she finally found the answer to her question. She had been wandering around the drawing-room, glancing into a book here, rearranging a vase of flowers there, turning over the pile of music on the piano, striking aimless chords on the harp-strings.

Presently she paused in front of the mantel to lift the lid from the rose-jar and let its prisoned sweetness escape into the room. As she did so she glanced up into the eyes of the portrait above her. With a whimsical smile she thought of the times before when she had come to it for counsel, and the question half-formed itself on her lips: " What would *you* do, you beautiful Grandmother Amanthis ? "

Instantly there came into her mind the memory of a winter day when she had stood there in the firelight before it, stirred to the depths by the music this one of " the choir invisible " had made of her life, by her purpose to " ease the burden of the world " — " to live in scorn of miserable aims that end with self."

Now like an audible reply to her question the

eyes of the portrait seemed to repeat that last sentence to her: "*To live in scorn of miserable aims that end with self!*"

For a moment she stood irresolute, then dropping the lid on the rose-jar again, she crossed over into the next room and sat down beside the library table. It was no easy task to write the note she had decided to send. Five different times she got half-way through, tore the page in two and tossed it into the waste-basket. Each attempt seemed so stiff and formal that she was disgusted with it. Nearly an hour passed in the effort. She could not write the real reason for breaking her engagement for the ride, and she could not express too much regret, or he would make other occasions she would have to refuse, if she followed out the course she had decided upon, to give Bernice no further occasion for jealousy. It was the most difficult piece of composition she had ever attempted, and she was far from pleased with the stiff little note which she finally slipped into its envelope.

"It will have to do;" she sighed, wearily, "but I know he will think I am snippy and rude, and I can't beah for him to have that opinion of me."

In the very act of sealing the envelope she hesitated again with Katie's words repeating themselves in her ears: " It's more than she would do for you, if you were in her place."

While she hesitated there came a familiar whistle from somewhere in the back of the house. She gave the old call in answer, and the next moment Rob came through the dining-room into the hall, and paused in the library door.

" I've made my farewells to the rest of the family," he announced, abruptly. " I met Betty and Mary down in the orchard as I cut across lots from home. Now I've got about five minutes to devote to the last sad rites with you."

" Yes, we're going on the next train," he answered, when her amazed question stopped him. " The family sprung the surprise on me just a little while ago. It seems the doctor thought grandfather ought to go at once, so they've hurried up arrangements, and we'll be off in a few hours, two days ahead of the date they first set."

Startled by the abruptness of his announcement, Lloyd almost dropped the hot sealing-wax on her fingers instead of the envelope. His haste seemed to communicate itself to her, for, springing up, she stood with one hand pressing her little signet ring into the wax, while the other reached for the stamp-box.

"I'll be through in half a second," she said. "This lettah should have gone off yestahday. If you will post it on the train for me it will save time and get there soonah."

"All right," he answered. "Come on and walk down to the gate with me, and we'll stop at the measuring-tree. We can't let the old custom go by when we've kept it up so many years, and I won't be back again this vacation."

Swinging the letter back and forth to make sure that the ink was dry, she walked along beside him. "Oh, I wish you weren't going away!" she exclaimed, forlornly. "It's going to be dreadfully stupid the rest of the summah."

They reached the measuring-tree, and taking out his knife and pocket-rule, Rob passed his fingers over the notches which stood for the many years they had measured their heights against the old locust. Then he held out the rule and waited for her to take her place under it, with her back against the tree.

"What a long way you've stretched up between six and seventeen," he said. "This'll be about the last time we'll need to go through this ceremony, for I've reached my top notch, and probably you have too."

"Wait!" she exclaimed, stooping to pick something out of the grass at her feet. "Heah's anothah foah-leaved clovah. I find one neahly every time I come down this side of the avenue. I'm making a collection of them. When I get enough, maybe I'll make a photograph-frame of them."

"Then you ought to put your own picture in it, for you're certainly the luckiest person for finding them I ever heard of. I'm going to carve one on the tree, here by this last notch under the date. It will be quite neat and symbolical, don't you think? A sort of 'when this you see remember me' hieroglyphic. It will remind you of the long discussions we've had on the subject since we read 'Abdallah' together."

He dug away in silence for a moment, then said, "It's queer how you happened to find that just now, for last night I came across a verse about one, that made me think of you, and I learned it on purpose to say to you — sort of a farewell wish, you know."

"Spouting poetry is a new accomplishment for you, Bobby," said Lloyd, teasingly. "I certainly want to hear it. Go on."

She looked down to thrust the stem of the clover through the silver arrow that fastened her belt, and waited with an expectant smile to hear what Limerick or nonsense jingle he had found that made him think of her. It was neither. With eyes fixed on the little symbol he was outlining on the bark of the tree, he recited as if he were reading the words from it:

> " Love, be true to her;
> Life, be dear to her;
> Health, stay close to her;
> Joy, draw near to her;
> Fortune, find what your gifts
> Can do for her.
> Search your treasure-house
> Through and through for her.
> Follow her steps
> The wide world over;
> You must! for here is
> The four-leaved clover."

" Why, Rob, that is *lovely!* " she exclaimed, looking up at him, surprised and pleased. " I'm glad you put that clovah on the tree, for every time I look at it, it will remind me of yoah wish, and — "

The letter she had been carrying fluttered to the ground. He stooped to pick it up and return it to her.

" That's the lettah you are to mail for me," she said, giving it back to him. " Don't forget it, for it's impawtant."

The address was uppermost, in her clear, plain hand, and she held it toward him, so that he saw she intended him to read it.

"Hm! Writing to Alex Shelby, are you?" he said, with his usual brotherly frankness, and a sniff that plainly showed his disapproval.

"It's just a note to tell him that I can't ride with him Thursday," she answered, turning away.

"Did you tell him the reason?" he demanded, continuing to dig into the tree.

"Of co'se not! How could I without making Bernice appeah ridiculous?"

"But what will he think of you, if you don't?"

"Oh, I don't know! I've worried ovah it until I'm neahly gray."

Then she looked up, wondering at his silence and the grave intentness with which he was regarding her.

"Oh, Rob, don't tell me, aftah all, that you think it was silly of me! I thought you'd like it! It was only the friendly thing to do, wasn't it?"

He gave a final dig with his knife, then turned to look down into her wistful eyes. "Lloyd Sherman," he said, slowly, "you're one girl whose friendship means something. You don't measure up very high on this old locust, but when it comes to doing the

square thing — when it's a question of *honor*, you
measure up like a man!"

Somehow the unwonted tenderness of his tone,
the grave approval of his smile, touched her in a
way she had not believed possible. The tears sprang
to her eyes. There was a little tremor in her voice
that she tried to hide with a laugh.

"Oh, Rob! I'm so glad! Nothing could make
me happier than to have you think that!"

They started on down to the gate together. The
only sound in all the late afternoon sunshine was the
soft rustling of the leaves overhead. How many
times the old locusts had watched their yearly part-
ings! As they reached the gate, Rob balanced the
letter on his palm an instant. Evidently he had
been thinking of it all the way. "Yes," he said,
as if to himself, "that proves a right to the third
leaf." Then he dropped the letter in his pocket.

Lloyd looked up, almost shyly. "Rob, I want
to tell you something. Even after that letter was
written I was tempted not to send it. I was sitting
with it in my hand, hesitating, when I heard yoah
whistle in the hall, and then it came ovah me like
a flash, all you'd said, both in jest and earnest, about
friendship and what it should count for. Well, it
was the old test, like jumping off the roof and

climbing the chimney. I used to say ' Bobby expects it of me, so I'll do it or die.' It was that **way** this time. So if I have found the third leaf, Rob, it was *you* who showed me where to look for it."

Then it was that the old locusts, watching and nodding overhead, sent a long whispering sigh from one to another. They knew now that the two children who had romped and raced in their shadows, who had laughed and sung around their feet through so many summers, were outgrowing that childhood at last. For the boy, instead of answering " Oh, pshaw!" in bluff, boyish fashion, as he would have done in other summers gone, impulsively thrust out his hands to clasp both of hers.

That was their good-by. Then the Little Colonel, tall and slender like Elaine, the Lily Maid, turned and walked back toward the house. She was so happy in the thought that she had found the golden leaf, that she did not think to look behind her, so she did not see what the locusts saw — Rob standing there watching her, till she passed out of sight between the white pillars. But the grim old family sentinels, who were always watching, nodded knowingly and went on whispering together.

THE END.